**FRIEDRICH SCHLEIERMACHER**
THE EVOLUTION OF A NATIONALIST

FRIEDRICH SCHLEIERMACHER
THE EVOLUTION OF A NATIONALIST

BY JERRY F. DAWSON |||||||||||||||||||||||||||||||||||||||||||

|||||||||||||||||||| UNIVERSITY OF TEXAS PRESS, AUSTIN & LONDON

Library of Congress Catalog Card No. 65–27535
Copyright © 1966 by Jerry F. Dawson
All Rights Reserved
Manufactured in the United States of America

To my sister, Barbara, who will never be able to read it,
And to my loving wife, Margie, whose inspiration made it worthwhile.

PREFACE

My decision to use the story of Friedrich Schleiermacher's development as a nationalist as the topic for this manuscript came as a result of a term paper presented in a research seminar at The University of Texas. The seminar, under the direction of R. John Rath, was designed to create in its participants an interest in outstanding European nationalists of the nineteenth century. Schleiermacher's phenomenal dedication to the task of unifying Germany in the face of almost insurmountable opposition was on the surface a "natural" object of research. However, I quickly learned that Schleiermacher was at the same time both widely quoted and virtually unknown. Every major study of nationalism referred to the famous Berlin preacher but hardly any of these sources contained definite information on his life or his influence. Many students of nationalism credited Schleiermacher with great sermons and tremendous nationalistic influence on his own contemporaries and with succeeding generations, but these scholars seldom attempted to make more than a superficial investigation into his background and life.

The paradox of a man so well known and so frequently quoted, and at the same time so untouched by historical research, presented both a challenge and a mystery. I quickly found that the dearth of knowledge concerning this man was not due to a lack of resource material, for Schleiermacher left a wealth of records revealing the intimate details of his personal life, his political career, his preaching ministry, and his service as a teacher. Most fortunately the bulk of these sermons and other writings was collected and published within a decade after his death in 1834. This thirty-one–volume collection bears the general title of *Sämmtliche Werke*[1] and is divided into three parts: *Predigten, Zur Theologie,* and *Zur Philosophie.*

The volumes in the part entitled *Predigten* contain a majority of the sermons which Schleiermacher had preached during the forty years he spent in service of the Reformed Church and the Evangelical Church in Prussia. Since he did not write his sermons in manuscript form, those in this collection either were written by others who listened to the sermons or were written from the notes which he had used in delivering the messages. Few of the sermons are dated in any way and seldom is the church in which the sermon was delivered indicated. The fact that only about

[1] Friedrich Schleiermacher, *Sämmtliche Werke.*

half of the sermons have a specific title also makes it difficult to refer to many of them in any consistent way.

The second part of the collected works contains a mass of theological writings. Here are Schleiermacher's books on theological problems, his pamphlets and tracts concerning questions in church government, and several of his discourses on fine points in theology.

The third part of the collection contains the author's philosophical works. In the main, these writings deal with classical philosophy or history, but they include also a number of papers which he read before the Royal Academy in Berlin, as well as voluminous lecture notes from the courses which he conducted in ethics, educational theory, and politics. The *Sämmtliche Werke* thus constitutes the chief source for material on Schleiermacher's life as a nationalist.

Published sources include, in addition to the material dealing with Schleiermacher's professional career, various collections of letters, which constitute a valuable source of knowledge concerning his life. Both outstanding and usable is a four-volume collection of Schleiermacher's letters entitled *Aus Schleiermachers Leben in Briefen,*[2] of which the first two volumes have been translated into English with excellent editorial notes by Frederica Rowan.[3] A more recent edition of Schleiermacher's letters was published by Heinrich Meisner in 1922.[4] Although most of the letters in the Meisner publication were sent to close friends and acquaintances, this two-volume work carries several valuable letters not included in the Reimer collection. Another group of letters was published by Herman Mulert[5] just after the Meisner edition appeared, but the Mulert single-volume collection is of considerably less importance than the other two. A collection of letters between Schleiermacher and Henrietta von Willich, whom he married in 1809, is also available.[6] A great many of these letters can be found in the other publications mentioned above, but the existence of this particular source of correspondence in a single volume is of considerable value.

All three of Schleiermacher's more notable books, *Reden über Religion, Monologen,* and *Glaubenslehre,* have been translated into Eng-

[2] Georg Reimer (ed.), *Aus Schleiermachers Leben in Briefen.*

[3] Friedrich Schleiermacher, *The Life of Friedrich Schleiermacher,* translated by Frederica Rowan.

[4] Heinrich Meisner (ed.), *Schleiermacher als Mensch: Sein Werden und Wirken, Familien-und Freundesbriefe.*

[5] Herman Mulert (ed.), *Briefe Schleiermachers.*

[6] Heinrich Meisner (ed.), *Friedrich Schleiermachers Briefwechsel mit seiner Braut.*

lish, though the German editions are readily available and quite read-
able. Of more value and importance than the English versions of his
books has been a volume of Schleiermacher's sermons translated by
Mary Wilson.[7] The value of the Wilson translation lies in the fact that a
great many of the sermons which she translated were from those volumes
of his sermons which are now very difficult to acquire.

In addition to the collections of Schleiermacher's general works, his
correspondence, and his sermons, numerous sources of information concerning his life and activities are found in the memoirs and letters of
other outstanding nationalists of his day. From these varied and numerous sources one seemingly should be able to draw an accurate picture of
the evolutionary development of Friedrich Schleiermacher as a nationalist.

The impetus to write this biography which came from the availability
of material for studying the life of the Berlin theologian was complemented by a pressing need for a better understanding of the phenomenon
of patriotism and its relationship to nationalism. With the surge of nationalism in the former colonial areas of Asia, Africa, and South America, an understanding of the source and the course of development of
experiences such as those of Schleiermacher seemed a necessity.

Most of the newly created nations of the world have experienced the
national enthusiasm which swept Germany during the Napoleonic era.
Though many dissimilarities exist between the experiences of the nineteenth centry and those of the twentieth, the dynamic personal determination by devoted individuals who are willing to sacrifice everything for
the good of the nation is still evident. The object of this investigation is
to try to determine as precisely as possible just what makes a man a nationalist. Perhaps by looking closely at Schleiermacher's life as he matured in his nationalism we will be able to understand the problems and
the course of development of contemporary nationalism.

I am deeply indebted to Professor R. John Rath, whose interest and
concern provided constant stimulation for investigation of nationalism
as well as Schleiermacher's role as a nationalist. I am also deeply grateful to Professor Boyd Shafer, whose criticism of this manuscript was of
invaluable help. In addition, the assistance of Miss Florrie Conway, li-
brarian of Van Howeling Memorial Library at Wayland Baptist College,
played a large part in the collection of the material for this manuscript.
For the constant encouragement they gave me during the course of my

[7] Friedrich Schleiermacher, *Selected Sermons of Schleiermacher,* translated by
Mary Wilson.

graduate study I am grateful to Professors Joe B. Frantz, Oliver Radkey, Harry Bennett, and Barnes Lathrop. A special word of thanks must go to Miss Marie Chaney, who spent endless hours typing and retyping drafts of this manuscript. I must also express thanks to the administration and trustees of Wayland Baptist College for their material interest in making the publication of this book a reality. To my wife, Margie, who has patiently endured the hardships of a manuscript wife, I express my heartfelt love.

CONTENTS

FRIEDRICH SCHLEIERMACHER
THE EVOLUTION OF A NATIONALIST

The growth and development of nationalism in the nineteenth century was one of the most important events in modern history. The alteration of the political structure of Europe on the basis of the concept of absolute personal loyalty to the nationality, or the nation, was so dynamic that most of the history of the world since the days of Napoleon hinges upon the national theme. Contemporary history is witness to the fact that in Asia, Africa, and Latin America the spirit of nationalism is the fundamental motivating factor in these former colonial areas. Because of its profound implications nationalism has been the object of intense study not only among those who want to know the course of man's past activities but also by persons who want to understand the ideas behind the powerful nationalist movements of today. Historians have hoped that a study of the sources of nationalistic feeling and the roles played by individuals in the growth of the concept of the nation will perhaps prevent the recurrence of the mistakes and ill effects of early nationalism.

One of the more difficult problems which arises in studying nationalism has been the difficulty of arriving at a satisfactory definition of the term "nationalism." Most historians, while admitting that nationalism has existed in amazingly varied forms, have not as yet been able to state specifically just what nationalism is. The dean of studies on nationalism, Carlton J. H. Hayes, perhaps closer to giving a complete and concise definition of the term than any other writer, said that nationalism was the phenomenon where:

...whole peoples have been systematically indoctrinated with the tenets that every human being owes his first and last duty to his nationality, that nationality is the ideal unit of political organization as well as the actual embodiment of cultural distinction, and that in the final analysis all other human loyalties must be subordinated to loyalty to the national state, that is, to national patriotism.[1]

[1] Carlton J. H. Hayes, *Essays on Nationalism,* p. 26.

In discussing the similarities between religion and nationalism Hayes
was even more specific in defining nationalism as the "fusion of patriotism with a consciousness of nationality."[2] Most subsequent attempts to
study or define nationalism have been conscious efforts to deal with the
subject without making the study a repetition of what Hayes had already
said. Some historians, like Boyd Shafer in his *Nationalism: Myth and
Reality*,[3] have avoided a concise definition of nationalism, choosing
rather to list characteristics which, individually or collectively, may create a sense of loyalty to a nationality. Others, like Louis L. Snyder in his
The Meaning of Nationalism, have been even less specific. Snyder sub-
divided nationalism and loyalty to the state into dozens of types of nationalism without ever really coming to a precise definition. Snyder
avoided an all-inclusive formula because he felt that nationalism was a
process or a combination of feelings and emotions, rather than a set of
fixed ideas which could be easily and accurately defined.[4] Still other
scholars have abandoned the general field of nationalism in order to concentrate on one of its particular aspects or on an outstanding national
leader. One of these authors, Hans Kohn, said in *Nationalism: Its Meaning and History* that nationalism was "a state of mind, in which the supreme loyalty of the individual is felt to be due the nation-state."[5]

Occasionally a writer approaches nationalism as though it were not
real at all. Elie Kedourie says in *Nationalism* that it is an artificial creation, an invention, which "pretends to supply a criterion for the determination of the unit of population proper to enjoy a government exclu-
sively its own, for the legitimate exercise of power in the state, and for
the right organization of a society of states."[6]

Each of these writers in his own way points out that nationalism, as a
subject of historical research, is a very complicated and intricate field of
inquiry. Because so many different views exist as to the definition of nationalism it is not surprising that there are so many different methods
of approaching the subject. Carlton J. H. Hayes established what might
be called the traditional approach when he wrote the first serious investigation of the subject of nationalism, *The Historical Evolution of Modern
Nationalism.*[7] He traced the ideas of outstanding men, showing how the
principles of nationalism slowly evolved into a dynamic way of life.

[2] Carlton J. H. Hayes, *Nationalism: A Religion,* p. 2.
[3] Boyd Shafer, *Nationalism: Myth and Reality,* pp. 7–8.
[4] Louis L. Snyder, *The Meaning of Nationalism,* pp. 4–6, 74–82, 146.
[5] Hans Kohn, *Nationalism: Its Meaning and History,* p. 9.
[6] Elie Kedourie, *Nationalism,* p. 9.
[7] Carlton J. H. Hayes, *The Historical Evolution of Modern Nationalism.*

Ergang's *Herder and the Foundations of German Nationalism*[8] and Pundt's *Arndt and the National Awakening in Germany*[9] followed the methods of Hayes, but they both applied their efforts to the study of an individual instead of a group of outstanding nationalists. Both of these authors were determined to show how nationalism came into being because of the steadfast devotion of men who were unique in their time. The other specialized works that have been written on nationalism since these books appeared have also followed Hayes' earlier pattern. Of course, the author may deal with a topic instead of a person, as was the case with Pinson in *Pietism as a Factor in the Rise of German Nationalism*[10] and Baron in his *Modern Nationalism and Religion.*[11] Even when authors approach nationalism from a tangent such as religion, however, these same historians ultimately revert to a description of the men who were responsible for the spread of the spirit of nationalism.

The chief weakness of the traditional approach to nationalism is that the author has seldom attempted to explain how the nationalist came to believe in the nation as the supreme object of his devotion. In most cases the historical narration begins with a statement that the nationalist in question became a nationalist because of the interaction of a number of different influences upon his life. The author then brings forth proof that his subject wrote on nationalistic themes or was involved in nationalistic activities. This approach does not reveal how the nationalist came to uphold the virtues of his nationality. Rather, the process by which he became a patriot is taken for granted. If one ignores the complex of events and circumstances which cause the nationalist to have a supreme allegiance to his nationality, then the true character of the nationalist cannot be clearly understood. By studying closely the various intellectual, spiritual, political, and personal experiences of an ardent defender of nationalism, one should be able not only to analyze the phenomenon of nationalism but also to see the nationalist as a unique creature who retained his identity though he cooperated in a selfless undertaking. From this point of view it would seem that a good definition of nationalism would be the process by which one maximizes his personal characteristics so that he has a dual identity. He sees himself as part of something "good" and at the same time rises above his own characteristics which may be "bad." Thus the nationalist sees the personification

[8] Robert Ergang, *Herder and the Foundations of German Nationalism.*
[9] Alfred G. Pundt, *Arndt and the National Awakening in Germany.*
[10] Koppel Pinson, *Pietism as a Factor in the Rise of German Nationalism.*
[11] Salo W. Baron, *Modern Nationalism and Religion.*

of all his desirable traits, as well as the desirable traits of his countrymen, in the nation. At the same time he is able to see in each man within the nation some of the superior traits which make up the national character. The perfect example of a man whose life presents a clear picture of the gradual development of this type of love of country was Friedrich Ernst Daniel Schleiermacher.

Few of the residents of Berlin had ever heard the name of the young chaplain of the Evangelical Hospital in that city in 1798, when Schleiermacher began his literary career. Within three years virtually every person of Protestant affiliation who had more than a passing interest in theology was either praising or condemning Schleiermacher's theological concepts. By the simple expedient of printing five short sermonettes in a text entitled *Über die Religion: Reden an die Gebildeten unter ihren Verächtern,* he became the most important figure in Protestant theology since the time of the Reformation.[12] Even today Schleiermacher is looked upon by most recognized authorities as a towering figure in the history of theology. Karl Barth, one of the world's most eminent theologians, has gone so far as to say that no theologian has yet answered Schleiermacher effectively and that contemporary Protestant theology is the child of Schleiermacher.[13] Robert Clyde Johnson, a rising young American Presbyterian, summarized the feelings of American theologians even better than Barth when he said, "Schleiermacher represented in theology what Kant had effected in philosophy. . . . In one quite definite sense, all contemporary Protestant theology . . . is a conversation with Schleiermacher."[14]

Schleiermacher's reputation as an outstanding theologian has tended to overshadow the fact that he was also a leading contributor to the growth of the spirit of nationalism in Germany. After the publication of *Über die Religion* in 1799, he spent as much time and effort in nationalistic activities as he did in the work of the ministry, perhaps more. But in spite of his involvement in political movements and nationalistic agitation, most of the attention given him by scholars has been in the field of religion. Theologians and philosophers have devoted a great deal of research to his contributions in the fields of ethics, theology, metaphysics, epistemology, and even education—all of which reflect his religious interests. Very little historical research has been centered on his importance

---

[12] Franz Schnabel, *Deutsche Geschichte im Neunzehnten Jahrhundert,* III, p. 115.

[13] Karl Barth, *Die protestantische Theologie im 19. Jahrhundert,* p. 380.

[14] Robert C. Johnson, *Authority in Protestant Theology,* p. 64.

as a contributor to German nationalism, and the little work that has been done on his nationalistic activities generally has been very limited in its scope. Thus far no historian has attempted to create from the rich experiences of Schleiermacher's life the story of the evolution of his nationalism.

The first historian to attempt any serious treatment of the Berlin theologian's life was Wilhelm Dilthey, who wrote an article entitled "Schleiermachers politische Gesinnung und Wirksamkeit," which appeared in the *Prussische Jahrbücher* in 1862.[15] The warm response to this article led Dilthey to enlarge upon the subject, and in 1870 the first volume of a proposed two-volume work on the life of Schleiermacher was published.[16] Unfortunately, Dilthey did not live to publish the second volume, which was to cover the years from 1806 until 1834. Thus the first and only biography of Schleiermacher did not even touch upon the period of his active participation in the national awakening in Prussia. Dilthey, however, did focus attention upon the Berlin theologian's participation in the romantic movement, which played an important part in his transition from rationalism to nationalism.

The identification of Schleiermacher with the romanticists was reinforced in 1870 by Rudolph Haym's intensive and noteworthy study of the romantic school.[17] However, nothing was written to describe him as anything other than a theologian and romanticist until 1899, when Joseph Reinhard dealt briefly with his patriotic activities as a minister of the Gospel.[18] So little attention was paid to him as a nationalist that Meinecke's comprehensive study of the genesis of the German national state, published in 1907, made no reference at all to the contributions of Schleiermacher to the growth of German nationalism.[19]

The year following the publication of Meinecke's study (1908), Johannes Bauer rescued Schleiermacher's political reputation from total obscurity by publishing a study of his patriotic activities based on sermons delivered during the War of Liberation.[20] Although Bauer's book was restricted to a very narrow field and said nothing concerning his

15 Wilhelm Dilthey, "Schleiermachers politische Gesinnung und Wirksamkeit," *Prussische Jahrbücher,* X (1862), 234–277; *Wilhelm Diltheys gesammlte Schriften,* XI, 6–39.

16 Wilhelm Dilthey, *Leben Schleiermachers.*

17 Rudolph Haym, *Die romantische Schule.*

18 Joseph Reinhard, "Friedrich Schleiermacher als deutscher Patriot," *Neue Jahrbücher für Pädagogik,* IV (1899), 345–360.

19 Friedrich Meinecke, *Weltbürgertum und Nationalstaat: Studien zur Genesis des deutschen Nationalstaates.*

20 Johannes Bauer, *Schleiermacher als politischer Prediger.*

earlier years as a minister and teacher, it nevertheless demonstrated that the outstanding theologian of the University of Berlin was also a man of major political significance. A decade after Bauer called attention to Schleiermacher's patriotic services on behalf of Prussia, Richard Volpers published a detailed study of Friedrich Schlegel's importance as a German nationalist.[21] Volpers intended to prove that Schlegel had been of greater worth in the building of the German nation than had Schleiermacher, but the net result of the publication was that both men had their nationalistic reputations enhanced.

The first truly significant research published after 1870 on his political theories, *Die Staatsphilosophie Schleiermachers*, suffered from the fact that its author, Georg Holstein, treated Friedrich as though he were a cold, hard statistic.[22] He paid no attention to Schleiermacher's life or to the relationship between his political concepts and the manner in which these concepts had evolved. Also, Holstein strained to make him seem in sympathy with principles of government which had been incorporated in the Weimar Republic and this distorted somewhat his interpretation of the Berlin scholar.

Much more objective than Holstein's treatment was the magnificent study by Paul Kluckhohn on the relationship between Schleiermacher and the romanticists, which was published in 1925.[23] The chief value of this study was the way in which he demonstrated the fact that each of the romanticists had adopted the tenets of romanticism as a temporary expedient in a transitional process. Each of these men had adhered to the romantic point of view while searching for a stable foundation upon which to build a philosophy of life. As in the case of Schleiermacher, each of these men finally abandoned romanticism in favor of some other philosophy of life. Kluckhohn thus called attention to one significant part of Schleiermacher's evolutionary development as a nationalist.

The last attempt before World War Two to examine the nationalism of the Berlin preacher was by Ernst Müsebeck in 1927.[24] Müsebeck intended to make a thorough study of his nationalism and the role which he played in the development of the concept of the German nation, but

[21] Richard Volpers, *Friedrich Schlegel als politischer Denker und deutscher Patriot.*

[22] Georg Holstein, *Die Staatsphilosophie Schleiermachers.*

[23] Paul Kluckhohn, *Persönlichkeit und Gemeinschaft: Studien zur Staatsauffassung der deutscher Romantik.*

[24] Ernst Müsebeck, *Schleiermacher in der Geschichte der Staatsidee und des Nationalbewusstseins.*

unfortunately his brief book degenerated into a lengthy comparison of Schleiermacher's work with that of Leopold von Ranke.

The scarcity of scholarly studies of Schleiermacher's nationalism has been compensated for in a small measure by his inclusion in some of the general works on nationalism which have already been cited, although he usually has been given very little attention even in these works. Hayes, for instance, devoted only one footnote to him in his monumental *The Historical Evolution of Modern Nationalism*.[25] Pinson's study of Pietism and German nationalism devoted considerable attention to him, but Pinson concentrated on his contributions to Pietism and only indirectly considered his nationalistic efforts. Anderson, in his study of the impact of nationalism upon Prussian culture,[26] showed the part played by Schleiermacher in the spiritual life of the Berlin intellectuals but said very little concerning his political significance.

Because of the slight attention he has received from historians the question arises as to why no one has yet published a thorough study of Schleiermacher's life as a nationalist. The answer to this question does not lie in a scarcity of primary material with which to work, for his letters, sermons, autobiography, lectures, and books have all been collected and published, and much of the material has even been translated into the English language. His obscurity in German history could perhaps be a reason offered for not studying his life, even though his prominence in theology should have made him a more, and not less, attractive object of study.

Most probably the greatest barrier to an intensive investigation of his life as a nationalist has been the fact that he did not present posterity with a neat system of thought with which to work. That he himself was aware that he would not be a system builder after the fashion of Kant, Fichte, or Spinoza was obvious in a letter which he wrote early in his career to his father, in which he said concerning such philosophical systems:

I do not think that I shall ever succeed in forming for myself a regularly developed system, in the framework of which I shall be able to solve every question that may come about in connection with all the previous knowledge that I may have acquired; but I have always felt that to investigate and test, and to listen patiently to every party and to all witnesses, are the only means by which

[25] Hayes, *Historical Evolution of Modern Nationalism,* p. 105 n.
[26] Eugene N. Anderson, *Nationalism and the Cultural Crisis in Prussia, 1806–1815.*

we can achieve a sufficient degree of certainty and, above all, a clear distinction between those matters on which we must adopt decided views, and which we can account for to ourselves and to others, and those which we may leave undecided without detriment to our happiness or our tranquillity. In this manner I remain a patient spectator of the physical struggles of the theological and philosophical athletes without deciding in favor of any or staking my liberty on the victories of either side; never failing, however, to learn something from both.[27]

He kept his promise not to become involved in creating a great following by founding some great school of thought. He generally looked upon his own writings as a means of clarifying his thoughts or imparting a theory to a small group of intimate friends. This unwillingness to commit his ideas to paper meant that if anyone wished to find his opinions on controversial political matters he would have to search hundreds of letters and other documents. If Schleiermacher had taken the time to spell out his political theories within the framework of a well-balanced philosophy, then he probably would have been studied as thoroughly as Kant, Fichte, Hegel, or Nietzsche.

Another difficulty which one encounters in trying to study Schleiermacher's life as a nationalist is his lack of confidence in himself. He was so afraid of criticism that he purposely refrained from stating his opinions unequivocally in most documents meant for public consumption. On one occasion, while commenting on the *Athenaeum,* edited by the two Schlegel brothers and containing works by the members of the romantic school, he went so far as to say that he found it most disagreeable to see anything he had written reproduced in print.[28] The basis for his obsessive fear of criticism from others was his seeming inability to express himself without being misunderstood. He revealed very clearly this side of his personality in a letter to his father in 1793, in which he said:

I get into the black books of everyone, and poor I—who have very seldom an opinion on any particular subject, and even less with reference to the whole party—I am looked upon by the democrats as a defender of despotism and a friend of routine, while the party of the more venturesome regard me as a politician who turns his coat according to the wind and keeps back his opinion because he has prudence. The royalists think I am a Jacobin and prudent people

[27] Schleiermacher to his father from Drossen, December 23, 1789, Georg Reimer (ed.), *Aus Schleiermachers Leben in Briefin,* I, 78–79.
[28] Schleiermacher to Henrietta Herz from Berlin, June 16, 1799, *ibid.,* p. 225.

think of me as a thoughtless person with a tongue too long for my mouth. In theology as well my fate has been the same for a long time.[29]

He felt that if he were to be misunderstood in small or trivial matters on which he felt he had expressed his views clearly, then the possibility was even greater that he would be misunderstood in major issues on which he might take a firm position. He had witnessed the ordeals of philosophers like Spinoza, who wrote comprehensively concerning the needs of mankind and then spent the rest of their lives defending their names as well as their theories. He simply did not choose to live that kind of life.[30] As a result of his dislike for being an object of misunderstanding and criticism he did his best throughout his life to remain hidden from the public. As late as 1813 he confessed to his wife that, in spite of his reputation, he had never presented a paper to a public gathering of scholars.[31] When he did manage to overcome his fears and publish a book or some lectures, he lived in dread of what the reaction would be, nearly to the point of illness.[32]

These insights into his personality should help explain why one must study his personal life before reaching any valid conclusions concerning the evolution of his nationalism. Schleiermacher once said of one of his works that the only way to avoid misconceptions about the book was for the reader to know the author as well as he knew the book.[33] The present volume, in a sense, is an attempt to conform to his request that one come to know him as a man before judging his ideas.

A close analysis of his life will show that his devotion to Prussia, and later to Germany, was the result of the cumulative influences of his intellectual, spiritual, social, political, and personal experiences. His nationalism did not arise in a vacuum. No single experience or set of experiences led him to see the value of subjecting the will of the individual in the state to the collective will of all the people comprising the nation. From the time of the first contact which Schleiermacher had with the

[29] Schleiermacher to his father from Schlobitten, February 14, 1793, *ibid.,* pp. 108–109.
[30] Schleiermacher to August Twesten from Berlin, July 5, 1815, Heinrich Meisner (ed.), *Schleiermacher als Mensch: Sein Werden und Wirken, Familien- und Freundesbriefs,* II, 223.
[31] Schleiermacher to Henrietta Schleiermacher from Berlin, June 24, 1813, Reimer (ed.), *Aus Schleiermachers Leben,* II, 300–301.
[32] Schleiermacher to Henrietta Herz from Berlin, July 5, 1799, *ibid.,* I, 230; Schleiermacher to Henrietta Herz from Berlin, March 5, 1799, *ibid.,* I, 202–203.
[33] Schleiermacher to Henrietta Herz from Berlin, March 5, 1799, *ibid.,* I, 202–203.

Pietists as a youth until he died in 1834 his life was a constant process of study, evaluation, readjustment, and compromise in the light of the events of everyday life. The most fundamental of all these experiences which contributed to making him a nationalist was the religious emotionalism he encountered as a student of Pietism.

As Hayes pointed out in *Nationalism: A Religion,* nationalism usually is an extension of the expression of religious emotionalism, or a substitute for it.[34] This is not to say that nationalism is actually a religion or that a person involved in swearing allegiance to the state is duplicating the experience of declaring his devotion to God. The degree to which one is willing to broaden the definition of religion will determine whether religious devotion and nationalism are identical. However, nationalism can quite easily be seen as a substitute for religion, or an outgrowth of it. Religion is so often the breeding ground for nationalism because one can relate it to national devotion more easily than to many other basic emotions. Nationalism also draws much strength from the Christian doctrine that a man cannot live unto himself, which the nationalist interprets to mean that only the nation offers an identity to the individual. Nationalism satisfies to some degree the innate desire for immortality by assuring man that the nation will bear his image long after he is dead. According to Hayes, nationalism "relates man to his nation's historic past and identifies him and his descendants with the future life of the nation. And its goal is the assurance of freedom and individuality and autonomy, if not to the person, at least to one's nationality and national state."[35]

What may be said of religious experience in general with reference to nationalism can be said much more specifically of Pietism. Pietism was a religious frame of mind or point of view which sought to change orthodoxy from the dead, rigid formality of eighteenth-century rationalism to a vibrant, living faith. A clear dichotomy had appeared in Protestant aims early in the eighteenth century in Europe, with one group in apparent agreement with the rationalists, who were demanding a review of doctrine in the light of Newtonian physics. This group wanted to alter religion in the hope that they could attract the intellectual by subjecting theology to the light of natural thought. Those of the other extreme were striving to achieve precisely the opposite effect. The Pietists felt that a quickening of the spiritual life of Protestantism would serve to correct any of the doctrines which had been weakened by compromise. The

[34] Hayes, *Nationalism: A Religion,* pp. 14–16.
[35] *Ibid., pp.* 15–16.

Pietists were concerned that religion should have a positive effect on the daily life of the individual, an influence which for them could be achieved only through acceptance of the basic doctrines of the Church as they had been traditionally interpreted.[36] By taking a stand on a reinterpretation of the doctrines of the Church in the light of tradition the Pietists also established themselves as being opposed to government interference.

S. W. Baron emphasized the political significance of the Pietists when he said in *Modern Nationalism and Religion*:

By teaching religious enthusiasm and the individual's mystic union with his Creator, Pietism not only salvaged German religious feeling from its threatening petrification under overweening state control, but also set the pattern for the national enthusiasm and irrationalism that was to color so deeply all German nationalist thinking in the nineteenth century.[37]

Koppel Pinson added his voice to that of Baron when he showed with meticulous care that under the influence of secularization the ideas which are basic to Pietistic emotionalism could be made to apply to the nationality.[38]

The doctrine of the new life, which came only as a result of the regeneration of the believer, could very easily be applied to the nation. In order to achieve the new life, one must study the word of God in the vernacular, which meant that the Pietists had to place a great deal of importance upon German literature and upon the use of the German language in education. When transferred to the secular realm the idea of a national language and literature became the unifying factor in the history of German nationalism.[39] Certainly not all German Pietists became nationalists, but the possibility was great that devoted adherents of the Pietist movement would see in their nationality an area in which to extend their religious feelings. All of these nationalistic characteristics of Pietism help to explain how Schleiermacher was so deeply affected during his youth by the Pietistic environment of his home.

From Friedrich Schleiermacher's birth in Breslau in 1768 he was subjected to a home life where the atmosphere was dominated by re-

---

[36] Hugh R. Mackintosh, *Types of Modern Theology*, pp. 11–15; Pinson, *Pietism as a Factor in the Rise of German Nationalism*, pp. 13–15; Samuel Peake, *Germany in the Nineteenth Century*, II, 134–135; Friedrich Schleiermacher, *Soliloquies*, pp. xiii–xiv.

[37] Baron, *Modern Nationalism and Religion*, p. 131.

[38] Pinson, *Pietism as a Factor in the Rise of German Nationalism*, pp. 135–151.

[39] *Ibid.*, pp. 141–146; Baron, *Modern Nationalism and Religion*, pp. 132–133.

ligious formalism. His father, Gottlieb, who was a regimental chaplain for the Reformed Church in the Prussian armies of Silesia, was constantly haunted by the knowledge that he preached from habit and not from conviction. After having tried in vain to find comfort in Quakerism, Pietism, and Wesleyanism, he was determined that his children should come to know the living faith, which somehow had always eluded him. For thirteen years he tried by means of a strong religious environment in the home to transmit to his son, Friedrich, the ideals of holiness and sanctity, which he himself had missed. When Gottlieb recognized in his son a skeptical attitude concerning the doctrines he wished to inculcate in him, he immediately made arrangements for him to attend the United Moravian Brethren's school at Niesky, where Schleiermacher matriculated in 1783.[40] His parents hoped that the Pietistic influence of the Moravians would enable him to overcome his doubts and conceit and at the same time give him companions better than those with whom he had been associating.[41]

As is true in many such cases, the intended cure for the son's troubles only deepened his difficulties. Instead of being impressed by the goodness of the Brethren, he accepted their doctrine of the natural sinfulness of all men. The shocking result was that he could not accept their claims for the supernatural experiences of Pietism.[42] Having discovered in himself a liking for the classics and Greek antiquity, he turned away from the rigorous doctrinal training of the Brethren by simply not attending classes. Strangely enough, in a school devoted to otherworldliness and the "inner light," Schleiermacher acquired a very profound interest in the physical world around him. He wanted to apply the doctrine of love to his environment instead of "using up" his emotions in activities which actually benefited no one. Before he had reached his eighteenth birthday he was beginning to make the transition from Pietism to the vague beginning of nationalism by acquiring a growing interest in the practical world of human affairs. This is not to say that he was pleased with his own scepticism, for he was deeply concerned lest he offend his father. After a long discussion with his father, Schleiermacher decided that he should move from Niesky to Barby, where the best of the Moravian seminaries was located. Even though he was obviously not psychologi-

---

[40] "Autobiography" in Reimer (ed.), *Aus Schleiermachers Leben,* I, 3–4; Dilthey, *Leben Schleiermachers,* pp. 3–12.

[41] Schleiermacher's mother to Uncle Stubenrauch [no place, no date], Reimer (ed.), *Aus Schleiermachers Leben,* I, 21–22.

[42] "Autobiography" in *ibid.,* pp. 6–7.

cally prepared for the doctrines of the Moravians he was willing to study for the ministry in order to please his father.

The only major result of his transfer to Barby in 1785 was an increase in his dissatisfaction with Pietistic doctrines. No longer able to stand the virtual confinement imposed upon him by his doctrinal studies he turned to reading secretly purchased volumes of poems by Goethe.[43] This forbidden literature not only increased his longing to delve more deeply into contemporary writings, but also strengthened his determination to break away from the Moravian school. Partly through the influence of an uncle named Stubenrauch, who lived in Halle, partly through theological contemplation, and partly out of his extreme personal unhappiness due to his lack of religious conviction, Schleiermacher wrote to his father in January, 1787, stating that he could no longer bear the company of the Moravians. He confessed to his father that he could not even accept the basic doctrine that Jesus Christ was the son of God, because Jesus had referred to Himself only as the son of man. Furthermore, the death of Jesus for the sins of the world was for him an impossibility, because Jesus Himself had never said that this was the reason He would die. And finally, Schleiermacher told his father that he could not accept the doctrines concerning eternal punishment, because God obviously did not create man with a capacity for perfection and thus could not eternally punish a man for being less than perfect.[44] The young sceptic told his father that with such unorthodox feelings in his heart he had only one recourse. He would leave Barby and enroll at the University of Halle, where he would be free to study mankind as a participant in history rather than as an intangible object of the wrath of God. "You have to realize that the success of my life depends upon this," pleaded the young scholar in a parting word of apology to his father.[45]

He left the Moravian seminary the next month with the dismayed consent of his father and enrolled at Halle in the fall of 1787.[46] Twelve challenging years later he confessed that, although he had encountered some very dynamic ideas and men since he had left Barby, Pietism had exerted a more profound influence upon his life than had any other philosophy or point of view. As he stated it:

[43] *Ibid.*, pp. 8–11; Uncle Stubenrauch to Schleiermacher from Halle, December 10, 1875, *ibid.*, p. 36.
[44] Schleiermacher to Gottlieb Schleiermacher from Barby, January 21, 1787, *ibid.*, pp. 42–43.
[45] *Ibid.*, pp. 44–45.
[46] Gottlieb Schleiermacher to Schleiermacher [no place, no date], *ibid.*, pp. 62–64.

Piety was the mother's womb in whose holy darkness my young life was fed and prepared for a world which was already sealed for it. In it my soul breathed before it had discovered its own place in wisdom and experience. It helped me when I began to sift the beliefs of my fathers and as I cleaned thought and feeling from the rubbish of the past. When God and the immortality of my childhood vanished from my criticizing eyes it remained with me.[47]

Pietism was thus the foundation upon which Schleiermacher constructed his approach to mankind, theology, philosophy, and ultimately nationalism. He evidenced a willingness to reject involved speculation concerning man's theoretical future and to concentrate on the day-to-day problems of existence. In leaving the Moravian school he cut himself loose from the doctrinal bonds of the Pietists but he retained the Pietistic consciousness of a dependence upon God. The retention of the emotionalism of the Pietists was probably the most important development in his growth as a nationalist, for nationalism itself is a highly emotional experience, defying logical processes and historical evidence. Once he had acquired the emotional predisposition to approach humanity's problems from the irrational, personalistic point of view, he had created a foundation upon which he could build the structure of nationalism.

[47] *Über die Religion* in Friedrich Schleiermacher, *Sämmtliche Werke, Zur Theologie,* I, 152.

||||||||| 2. SCHLEIERMACHER, RATIONALISM, AND ROMANTICISM

The subtle, subjective influence of Pietism upon Schleiermacher was an excellent preparation for the next step he took in his evolutionary progress toward nationalism: the study of rationalism. When he cast off the yoke of rigid Moravian Pietistic doctrines in order to study at Halle, he did more than just leave one institution for another. He cut himself off from a basic interpretation of the relationship of man to God and of man to society. Discarding his theological interpretation of human relations necessitated a vigorous search for a suitable substitute with which he would be able to evaluate society. Almost accidentally he turned to reading the works of the great German philosopher, Immanuel Kant, in the hope that in Kant he might find a suitable substitute for the moral absolutism of the Moravians, which he had just discarded. After having read Kant's *Prolegomena* the young scholar was sure that he was ready for a detailed study of Kantian metaphysics and ethics before he ever arrived at the University of Halle.[1] Though not exactly positive that he understood all that was involved in Kantian rationalism, he was still captivated by the philosopher's unusual approach and methodology. The big surprise came for the young scholar when he arrived at Halle and found that Kantian rationalism was not a popular subject among the professors at the University. Possibly as a continuation of his rebellious attitude at Barby, or in defiance of his professors, but more probably because of his consistent aversion to accepting intricate ideas without first investigating them, Schleiermacher from the moment he arrived in Halle buried himself in Kantian thought in order to defend the philosopher from the attacks of his Halle professors.[2] However, even though he made an intensive study of Kant's philosophy, he did not

---

[1] Gottfried Schleiermacher to Friedrich Schleiermacher [no place, no date], Georg Reimer (ed.), *Aus Schleiermachers Leben in Briefen,* I, 62–63.

[2] Friedrich Schleiermacher to his father from Halle, August 14, 1787, *ibid.,* I, 65–66; Wilhelm Dilthey, *Leben Schleiermachers,* I, 39–46; Friedrich Schleiermacher, *Soliloquies,* pp. xviii–xix.

become a devoted follower as so many of the philosophy students did during the last two decades of the eighteenth century. He saw within the Kantian system too many disagreeable philosophical complications that prevented it from answering the specific problems of man.

To be more specific, the categorical imperative, the demand by Kant that man regulate his moral values on the basis of what the moral act would mean if everyone in the community committed it, was too vague to be of real value. Schleiermacher was much more attracted by Kant's advocacy of the freedom of rational process for the individual than by his ethical theories. He could readily see from his Pietistic point of view that individuality not only qualified one to approach God without help from an outside source, but also qualified one to interpret moral acts according to the way these acts would affect the community. Until he studied Kant, however, he had never been able to see any way to justify the personal evaluation of moral acts in the light of what effect the moral decision would have.

His ability to see a justification for individuality in Kant's philosophy was one of the more important intellectual achievements in his development toward nationalism. The most vital factor in his concept of nationalism, the belief in the possibility of expressing the collective will of all the people by teaching the traditions of the nationality, rested ultimately upon the possibility of expressing an individual will in any manner. Once he had extracted this kernel of rationalism from Kantian philosophy he was well on his way toward an interpretation of the individual as a political as well as a moral agent within the state.

Quite significantly Schleiermacher had been able to retain from Kantian rationalism only one useful philosophical concept, the unique moral responsibility of the individual, just as he had utilized only a small but vital part of Pietism. He had been so little affected by Kant that when he had an opportunity to spend several hours with the famous philosopher in Königsberg, Schleiermacher left the meeting totally unimpressed.[3]

Kant did not deserve all the credit for leading Schleiermacher to see the value of individual expression within the framework of society. Another philosopher who contributed a great deal to his evolution as a nationalist by focusing attention upon the importance of the individual was Spinoza. From 1793 until 1796 Schleiermacher studied Spinoza's theories with even more concentration than he had devoted to Kant. As

[3] Schleiermacher to his father from Schlobitten, May 15, 1791, Reimer (ed.), *Aus Schleiermachers Leben,* I, 87–88.

a result of his intensive study of the works of Spinoza he wrote two excellent essays on Spinoza's system of philosophy of individualism: "A Description of Spinoza's System" and "Spinozianism." Since Spinoza's works had not been published by 1795, Schleiermacher based both of these writings on Friedrich Jacobi's *Letters concerning the Theories of Spinoza.*

Although he was deeply impressed by Spinoza's concept of substance and universal order, Schleiermacher believed that the defects of his system outweighed its merits. Spinoza belittled human passion and will, which, because of his Pietistic background, Schleiermacher valued very highly. Also, in Spinoza's system individuality was equated with limitation. Spinoza could not visualize any logical activity which would have meaning beyond the limited confines of personal activity. Having already accepted Kant's view that the moral will was man's absolute dignity, not his source of limitation, Friedrich rejected Spinoza's insistence that the individual was limited in his activities to purely self-related functions.

In the process of disputing with Spinoza, he realized an aspect of individuality which he had not yet seen. He discovered that the individual truly lived in a world of individual acts and functions, while still maintaining a group identity. This enabled the individual to retain his personal freedom and individuality even though each free individual act was a part of a group action. While he exercised his freedom the individual might think that his free act had no limitation, but the force of tradition and public opinion would so mold his act that it would not in a true sense be free.[4]

Although it is difficult to determine the relative values of the influences of Kant and Spinoza upon Schleiermacher, one must admit that without their contributions his development as a nationalist would certainly have been different. One must also remember that neither Kant nor Spinoza gave him a satisfactory explanation of man's relationship to his fellow man. His still unresolved goal remained the finding of a "world view which does justice to human personality, on the one hand, and to the infinite universe that stands over against man, on the other."[5]

Schleiermacher's adventures in the realm of philosophical speculation never made him oblivious to the world of events around him, but the steady intellectual progress he was making toward a nationalistic point of view was not matched by an ability to make practical applica-

[4] Richard Brandt, *The Philosophy of Schleiermacher,* pp. 35–38; Schleiermacher, *Soliloquies,* pp. 121–126.
[5] Schleiermacher, *Soliloquies,* p. xxiii.

tions of his ideas. Three or four brief glances at his writings and letters demonstrate clearly that by 1795 his concept of patriotism was still a very weak conviction, although he was beginning to recognize in a very immature way the value of national traditions. One of the documents which reveals this weak but nevertheless noticeable spirit of nationalism is a letter which Friedrich wrote to his father concerning the progress of the French Revolution through the year 1793. In this letter he admitted that on the whole he had heartily sympathized with the French people during the first three years of the revolution. He was quick to add that just because he thought that the revolution was good for France, this did not mean that he was "seized by the foolishness of wanting to imitate it" in Germany.[6] Here was the faint beginning of a consciousness of the role which tradition must play in the life of any group of people. He did not think that the French Revolution was "wrong" for France because the revolutionary spirit obviously arose out of the historical processes and developments of the French nation. The French Revolution would be "wrong" for Germany because the German people had experienced none of the phenomena that had led to the overthrow of the Ancient Regime in France. In other words, he defended the French Revolution on the basis of his belief that the French people were expressing their national feelings. He then denied the possibility of the same type of revolution for Germany on the grounds that such a revolution in Germany would be completely out of character for the German people. The difficulty inherent in this point of view was that the people with whom he conversed concerning the Revolution did not share his ideas on the historical progress of national groups. Consequently, most of his close associates leaped to the false conclusion that he was a defender of the spirit of revolt.[7]

Schleiermacher derived a valuable lesson from the criticism which his defense of the French Revolution aroused: one must be precise when speaking about nationalities. He could see that people were motivated less by reason and more by emotion when it came to national problems than in most other areas of their social life. He also came to see that people who were strong in their national devotion could seldom see the value of the nationalism of people of other nationalities. Every time Schleiermacher tried to point out to his friends that Frenchmen were entitled to actions consistent with their historical heritage, he found that

[6] Schleiermacher to his father from Schlobitten, February 14, 1793, Reimer (ed.), *Aus Schleiermachers Leben,* I, 107–109.
[7] *Ibid.,* I, 109.

they immediately misunderstood him. "Such has been my fate in relation to French affairs more than a thousand times," he said to his father
in 1793.[8]

A second document revealing his growing but still immature sense of
nationalism in the early 1790's is a sermon which he delivered late in
1793 or early in 1794. In this undated and untitled sermon he repeated
what he had said on other occasions about the French Revolution, but
he revealed a more mature approach to the national sensibilities of his
German listeners by emphasizing German traditions instead of praising
what the French had done. He explained that the Revolution had been
for the French a natural result of a long series of events which they had
experienced as a nation. In the sense that contemporary events in France
were the rational outgrowth of historical developments, they were correct and necessary. This was the same approach that he had used before
in describing the French Revolution. The difference came when he very
carefully called attention to the fact that the hallowed traditions of
Germany, sanctioned by the German people since the days of Martin
Luther, would not allow the Germans to make the foolish mistake of
trying to copy the example of France. Schleiermacher seemed to be a
polished nationalist when he declared, in an appeal to the emotions of
his listeners, that if Germans ever encountered the problems which had
driven the French into a revolution, the spirit of German tradition would
almost certainly force them to seek a peaceful solution to their problems.[9]

Since Luther's day the German people had adhered to the principle
of obedience to the law of the land and had maintained a respect for
each man's station in life. A man's pride in his own importance to society
because of his worthwhile occupation would not only make him a better
father and husband, but also would make him a firm believer in the
political system which allowed him to maintain his occupation. Schleiermacher felt that a man would never advocate revolution unless he
reached the point where he felt that his opportunities for personal recognition and advancement were being denied him by his government. Thus
he did not believe that the German tradition of obedience to the law
would prevent any type of revolution from occurring. He was saying
that there would not be a revolution of the French variety as long as the

---

[8] *Ibid.*
[9] Unnamed and undated sermon, Friedrich Schleiermacher, *Sämmtliche
Werke, Predigten,* II, 148–161.

German people had faith that their governments were being fair to them.[10]

The documents mentioned above indicate quite clearly that Schleiermacher possessed that kernel of nationalism, a faith in the traditions of a national group, long before he was able to make specific applications of any particular set of traditions. Hans Kohn called attention to an interesting aspect of nationalism when he said, "German nationalism—as all non-Western nationalism—was born in the war against France, not in an attempt to secure better government, individual liberty, and due process of law, but in an effort to drive out a foreign ruler and to secure national independence."[11] While this may be true, one should note that the nationalist often had the foundation of nationalism long before the structure had been erected. Without the many almost intangible and obscure concepts such as Schleiermacher revealed in his writings before the struggles of the first decade of the nineteenth century erupted between France and Germany, he might never have become the ardent patriot of a decade later. For instance, he used the terms "German" and "Germany" so loosely that one has to conclude that he had no clear conception of what constituted a German nation and that he was using generalities for the sake of argument. He was actually dealing with nationalism more or less in a philosophical sense rather than in a framework which could be applied to any specific group of people composing the German nation. In his opinion the religious nature of the Germans gave strength to the concept of submission to exterior authority. If God was the author of peace and if each man accepted the principle of peace in Kantian fashion, the leaders of Germany, who presumably had accepted the same principles as the people, would allow the free unfolding of the historical development of the people.

Although recognition of the value of tradition was a worthwhile and significant segment of Schleiermacher's nationalism, belief in the value of tradition was not, in and of itself, nationalism. He still lacked the insight or maturity to apply what he knew and felt in his heart to the world of practical events. Of course, he was not the first to encounter the difficulty of transmitting ideas and feelings into worthwhile political activity, nor would he be the last. He simply had reached the point

[10] Unnamed and undated sermon, *ibid.*, II, 116–120; Ernst Müsebeck, *Schleiermacher in der Geschichte der Staatsidee und des Nationalbewusstseins*, pp. 23–24.

[11] Hans Kohn, "Arndt and the Character of German Nationalism," *American Historical Review*, LIV (July, 1949), 789.

where he needed some help in making practical use of his nationalistic feelings. Fortunately for him, he came in contact with a group of Germany's more outstanding intellectuals, who were able through their stimulating environment and personal encouragement to help him work out his nationalistic ideas with coherence and force. These intellectuals who came to mean so much to his nationalistic career but who themselves were not nationalists were known as the "romanticists."

Schleiermacher was introduced into the romanticists' circle quite by chance. He had tutored the children of Alexander von Schlobitten for two years after he completed his education at Halle in 1789. Through Alexander he came to know Henrietta Herz, the beautiful and cultured wife of a Berlin doctor. Henrietta's home was the meeting place for a weekly social gathering of some of Berlin's more notable political and cultural figures, who devoted their meetings to discussions of literary works and to readings of essays.[12] Friedrich was not able to take immediate advantage of his newly acquired friendship with the scholars of the Herzes' circle because he was appointed by the Reformed Church to a pastorate in Landsberg in 1794. It was only in 1796, when he returned from Landsberg to Berlin as pastor of the Charity Hospital, that he became intimately associated with a particular set of Henrietta Herz's friends who were known as the romanticists. No other group of people made as great a contribution to the development of his nationalism as did these men. Even though few of them could be described as nationalists except in a very superficial way, they breathed into him a compassion for the homeland that he had never known during the course of his philosophical or theological wanderings.

Each of the romanticists left his own unique imprint upon Schleiermacher's life in such a way that he learned fundamental truths concerning nationalism from them without ever losing his own identity because of their influence. The member of the group who exercised the greatest influence in the realm of Schleiermacher's political thought was Novalis, a man with unusual talent for communicating intricate political ideas. When Schleiermacher was with him he sensed that Novalis was saying what he himself had wanted to say for a number of years and yet had never been able to express intelligently. Listening to Novalis expound on the virtues of the *Volk* and on the need for Germans to become a united people led Schleiermacher to crystallize his feelings on German

[12] Schleiermacher to his sister from Berlin, October 22, 1797, Reimer (ed.), *Aus Schleiermachers Leben*, I, 160–164.

traditions.[13] Novalis was thus probably more influential than any other man in getting Schleiermacher to see the need to apply nationalistic principles to all of Germany. Novalis used the organic concept of the state to show him the need for a clearer definition of Prussia's relationship with the rest of Germany. Novalis insisted that whether a people constituted a monarchy, an aristocracy, or a democracy, in the late-eighteenth-century sense of these terms, they must attempt to organize their nation as an organic whole. Schleiermacher had reached the same general conclusions about the need for individual recognition as a result of his philosophical speculations concerning Spinoza and Kant, but he had not realized the potentialities of individualism as an element of nationalism until he met Novalis. Thus, while Novalis was not the father of Schleiermacher's basic belief concerning the organic nature of the state, he did help him clarify his thoughts.[14]

The inspiration which Schleiermacher received from Ludwig Tieck, another member of the romanticist circle, was quite different from that which he acquired from Novalis. Where Novalis would show a direction or course for Schleiermacher's thought, Tieck would supply the desire to pursue the course. Friedrich's sense of inferiority—perhaps his greatest limitation as far as writing was concerned—somehow took a secondary place in his personality when he was in the presence of this great German writer. He once told a friend that Tieck was a man destined to occupy a position in the literature of Germany "which neither Goethe, nor Schiller, nor Richter, nor, perhaps any one but himself could fill."[15] The confidence which he felt for Tieck bolstered his own ego, for when he was in Tieck's presence he felt that he ought to express the ideas which he had within him, even if doing so should cause the world to laugh at him. Tieck did not convey any political concepts to Schleiermacher which could be interpreted as a contribution to his growth as a nationalist, but had it not been for him Schleiermacher might never have attempted to write the works in which he expressed nationalistic concepts.

If Novalis helped Schleiermacher discover a fundamental element of nationalism within himself, and if Tieck imparted to him the inspiration to share these discoveries with the world, then it must also be said that Wilhelm Schlegel gave to him the spark of determination to carry

---

[13] Paul Kluckhohn, *Persönlichkeit und Gemeinschaft: Studien zur Staatsauffassung der deutscher Romantik*, p. 55.

[14] *Ibid.*, pp. 55–58.

[15] Schleiermacher to Henrietta Herz from Berlin, July 1, 1799, Reimer (ed.), *Aus Schleiermachers Leben*, I, 227–229.

through to completion the lengthy journalistic undertakings which contained his nationalistic philosophy. Wilhelm was not the most important of the romanticists, but he made up with tenacity what he lacked in ingenuity. Because of his unique ability to remain at a task until it was completed Schlegel became an inspiration to Schleiermacher, who suffered from an inability to concentrate on a single manuscript over a long period of time.[16] The impact of Schlegel's determination was a significant factor which enabled Schleiermacher to write a number of works, both while he was with the romanticists and years after he had parted company with them.

Great though their influence was in helping him express his nationalist views in a coherent way, neither Tieck, Novalis, nor Wilhelm Schlegel had as much direct influence over Schleiermacher's eventual nationalistic outlook as did Wilhelm's brother, Friedrich Schlegel. Schleiermacher's relationship with the other romanticists was only casual in comparison with the close friendship which he established with him. This intimate acquaintance was important for the development of Schleiermacher's nationalism because it was through Schlegel that he came to know the personal satisfaction which the romanticists derived from the study of antiquity.

Carlton J. H. Hayes said that romanticism, together with forces created by the French Revolution and the Industrial Revolution, not only made the nationalistic process possible, but almost made the awakening of nationalism inevitable.[17] The romanticists' interest in folk language resulted in a widespread study of national philology. The natural result of these studies was the development of a deep-seated interest during the nineteenth century in national history.[18] To a small degree through Novalis, but more through Friedrich Schlegel than anyone else, Schleiermacher was exposed to a lively interest in antiquity—an interest which complemented his own scholarly studies in Greek philosophy.[19] Again, almost fortuitously, Schleiermacher's encounter and involvement with the romanticists came at a stage in his development as a nationalist when he could use their inspiration and interests to mature his nascent nationalism. From the day when he met Friedrich Schlegel in 1797 until the two men parted company approximately three years later Schleier-

[16] Schleiermacher to Henrietta Herz from Potsdam, February 25, 1799, *ibid.*, I, 198–200.
[17] Carlton J. H. Hayes, *Essays on Nationalism*, p. 59.
[18] *Ibid.*, p. 54.
[19] Friedrich Meinecke, *Weltbürgertum und Nationalstaat: Studien zur Genesis des deutschen Nationalstaates*, pp. 69–73.

macher was entranced by Schlegel. He readily admitted that Schlegel was the most stimulating individual that he had ever met, and that just being near Schlegel was an inspirational experience for him.[20] It was Schlegel who opened the world of romanticism to him, for it was he who introduced him to Tieck, Novalis, and Wilhelm Schlegel. It was Friedrich Schlegel who made him feel the joy of true friendship for the first time in his life. In fact, the two men were so devoted to one another that for a short while they shared a Berlin apartment.

The immediate consequence of this friendship between the two men was their attempt to translate the works of Plato.[21] This gigantic effort not only intensified Schleiermacher's desire to write and publish material resulting from his studies of Plato and antiquity in general, but also provided a means whereby Schlegel could impart to Schleiermacher the romantic tendency to idealize the past. The fact that Schlegel soon grew tired of translating Plato's works and moved on to other projects became insignificant in the light of the impulse toward glorification of a nation's past which he had imparted to Schleiermacher. This impulse was soon intensified into a compelling force as Schleiermacher cultivated his relationship with the other romanticists. He was quickly approaching that place in his nationalistic development where he would have to give expression to the feelings and emotions, as well as the philosophical concepts, which his associations with the romanticists had stirred within him.

The romanticists were quick to notice that Schleiermacher had reached an intellectual crisis in his life, and it was partly out of a desire to stimulate his self-expression that they began the publication of a cultural journal which they named the *Athenaeum*. After they had begun the journal they encouraged him to contribute articles in the hope that he would be able to "find himself." What they actually did do was bring Schleiermacher to the point where he would publish a book that denied the basic tenets of romanticism, and at the same time set forth his first clearly defined ideas on nationalism.

[20] Schleiermacher to his sister from Berlin, December 31, 1797, Reimer (ed.), *Aus Schleiermachers Leben*, I, 169–171.

[21] Schleiermacher to Henrietta Herz from Potsdam, April 29, 1799, *ibid.*, I, 169–171. Although it has no bearing on the rest of this manuscript it is interesting to note that Schleiermacher devoted a vast amount of his time after 1810 to studies in Greek philosophy. Of the twenty-three papers which he read before the plenary sessions of the Royal Academy of Science in Berlin from January, 1811, until August, 1832, in eight he discussed problems involving the works of Greek philosophers and in six others he compared in some way contemporary and Greek classical thought. These are listed and dated in Schleiermacher, *Sämmtliche Werke, Zur Philosophie*, III, xiii.

The issue which played a crucial part in causing him to lash out at the romanticists was religion. As far as the romanticists were concerned, from 1795 until the fall of Napoleon, religion was part of the cultural limitation that Germany's people needed to overcome. Later, the romanticists were to play a big part in the revival of Catholicism. Although the romanticists could possibly be described as "religious men" in 1795, for them religion was in its true sense an inward activity and the only inspiration which they recognized was the inspiration which led men to do good.[22] From the time Schleiermacher had met the romanticists he had struggled with the problem of trying to show these intellectual friends that they were wrong in attacking religion. Though none of the romanticists ever made light of the fact that he was a minister, he was able to feel the tension which his beliefs caused whenever he was among them. It is easy to see why Schleiermacher decided to use the subject of religion as his point of departure when the romanticists became insistent that he contribute to the *Athenauem* in order to clear up his personal problems and his difficulties in self-expression. But to the disappointment of the romanticists, he decided to write out his arguments in the form of a book instead of using the *Athenauem,* giving as his reasons for doing so the fact that he had few friends and as a result had never developed a talent for saying anything briefly. Since he lacked the ability to express himself in brief letters and short articles, his only alternative was to write a book.[23]

For the study of the growth of Schleiermacher's nationalism the book which he wrote, *Speeches on Religion to Its Cultured Despisers,* is a key document. To be sure, in the book he was attempting to correct the misunderstandings of the romanticists concerning religion and the connection between religion in its pure state and the Church, its imperfect embodiment. In the process of explaining the true nature of the Church to the romanticists he became involved in discussions concerning the people who are served by the Church and concerning the relationship of the Church to the state. He found that he could not discuss the role of the Church in Germany without discussing the principles of education utilized by the Church. This took him directly to the problems which became the battleground of nineteenth-century nationalism: education, the relations between citizens and the state, the importance of the use

---

[22] Erwin Kircher, *Philosophie der Romantik,* p. 5.

[23] Schleiermacher to Georg von Brinckmann from Berlin, March 22, 1800, Heinrich Meisner (ed.), *Schleiermacher als Mensch: Sein Werden und Wirken, Familien-und Freundesbriefe,* I, 167.

of German as a language, and the role of tradition in Germany. Since his *Speeches on Religion to Its Cultured Despisers* contained a vast amount of material on his early nationalism, and since he so very carefully explained himself in detail, this book commands the attention of the student of his nationalism.

Before discussing the contents of his book, one must note that Schleiermacher was well aware of the fact that some of his ideas would prove to be so distasteful to officials of the Reformed Church that his career would suffer from their publication. Thus the writing of the book put him under a severe psychological strain,[24] which in turn caused him to study his subject very carefully before he committed himself in print. Schleiermacher's statements on nationalism were consequently not off-hand remarks casually introduced into a discussion of religion. They were rather a studiously interwoven series of comments which were relevant to the author's concept of man's relationship to other men as well as man's relationship to God. An understanding of the pressure under which he worked will not only reveal the courage he demonstrated in writing the book, but will also give insight into the conviction he had on political and religious questions.

The study of Schleiermacher's *Speeches on Religion* must begin with an analysis of a philosophical or theological point so that the nationalistic implications can be understood. Friedrich's announced purpose in writing the *Speeches on Religion* was to show the romanticists that they criticized religion because they were ignorant of what actually constituted true religion. The type of religion which he held forth for them was not like the traditional religious systems of the German states, built as they were around dogmas. In place of dogmatic systems he offered them a religion like that of the Moravians, grounded in a personal relationship with a personal devotion to a personal God. He actually abandoned

---

[24] The tension under which Schleiermacher worked as he wrote *Speeches on Religion* was so great that he neglected not only the trivial activities of daily life but also some very important duties and responsibilities. The result was that he often did things during this time which were a source of extreme embarrassment to him. On one occasion he happened to pass Friedrich Wilhelm III while taking a walk, but Schleiermacher was so deeply engrossed in contemplation over his book that he paid the sovereign such little mind that he did not even remove his hat. A guard promptly stopped Schleiermacher and gave him a stern lecture on the respect due the head of state. See Schleiermacher to Henrietta Herz from Potsdam, March 20, 1799, Reimer (ed.), *Aus Schleiermachers Leben,* I, 204–205.

objective manifestations of worship and devoted his work to a subjective investigation into the religious frame of mind.[25]

The first logical step taken by him in his efforts to demonstrate the true nature of religious activity to the romanticists was to differentiate between religion and religious objects, between practical and theoretical religion. He felt that mankind had made the mistake of equating religious truths with outward manifestations of religion, such as the physical church. The same error had often been made in equating religious truths with the exact opposite of the physical church, Pietistic emotionalism. Followers of each of these tendencies had generally ridiculed and denounced the other due to the fact that people had by nature grown accustomed to either the theoretical side of religion, which produces a way of thinking, an attitude of contemplation, and specific feelings and desires, or to the practical side, which emphasizes a special type of conduct or morality. Schleiermacher was perfectly willing to accept the idea that both extremes of religious practice were a part of the religious life of Germany, but he emphatically denied that either purely practical or purely theoretical religion was in itself "true" religion.[26]

In order to prove to the romanticist that true religion was not to be found in religious ceremonies or in Pietistic emotionalism, he used an extremely interesting nationalistic interpretation of the role of the church. In Schleiermacher's opinion the outward manifestations of either religious point of view had always become associated with political attempts to preserve it, either by giving the Church a legal position in the state or by the state's assuming a legal position over the Church. Even people like the romanticists, who did not believe in the doctrines of the Church, were willing to let the Church set the moral standards of the nation, but not as a result of any sense of religious enthusiasm or dedication, nor of a belief in a specific set of theological doctrines. Even though the romanticists denied the validity of the doctrines of the Church, they were willing to grant to the Church the continued right to exist because of its usefulness. Schleiermacher rejected outright the idea that the Church should be allowed to exist solely because it functioned in such a way that the state realized a benefit from its presence. As

[25] *Über die Religion* in Schleiermacher, *Sämmtliche Werke, Zur Theologie,* I, 143–167; Franz Schnabel, *Deutsche Geschichte im neunzehnten Jahrhundert,* III, 116–118.
[26] *Über die Religion* in Schleiermacher, *Sämmtliche Werke, Zur Theologie,* I, 174.

Schleiermacher stated his case, "Could there exist a legal constitution which rests on piety? Would not the entire idea that you hold so sacred disappear as soon as you took such a point of view?"[27] In the first place, a relationship between Church and state based upon ecclesiastical utility would actually prove that the Church was a synthetic social force. In addition, Schleiermacher pointed out that the state did not need an institution like the Church as it was conceived by the romanticists because moral laws were the result of the traditions of the people as codified by the state. Here he touched upon the fundamental truth underlying the nationalist's devotion: that the people actually make the laws by maintaining linguistic or cultural traditions which ultimately are sanctioned by the state. To be sure, the Church as an institution played a leading part in shaping the traditions of the people, but the influence of that institution was effective only to the extent that it was able to kindle the spirit of true religion within the heart of its communicants. While the Church might exercise an influence upon tradition, true religion functioned as part of the tradition itself, at least in Germany. Schleiermacher thus quite effectively introduced the nationalistic theme into his defense of religion against the attacks of the romanticists.

Schleiermacher's discussion of the role of the Church in the life of the individual brought up for investigation another point relating to religion which had nationalistic implications. He was deeply concerned over a mistaken notion of the romanticists that theologians claimed to have a special type of knowledge which lay beyond the realm of reason. He contended that religion in itself was not knowledge of either the world or God, nor was it a science concerning them. Rather, religion was an affection where the infinite was felt and seen by the finite.[28]

Having attacked the romanticist's notion of Christian epistemology he felt compelled to demonstrate to them the exact nature of a Christian system of knowledge, although in doing so he had to turn to nationalistic proofs. His theory was in the nature of a triad in which the Ego, or the interior man, was the key component. The outer world, call it mass, matter, element, or form, was the opposite of the Ego. There was a coming together of the two elements and from this union, which was in constant change, a new state arose which perceived the absolute unity of both elements. This perception was knowledge as far as the individual was concerned. Schleiermacher moved quickly to apply this theory to the life of the individual when he said that the most significant problem

[27] *Ibid.*, I, 165.
[28] *Ibid.*, I, 184–185.

for the Ego was transmitting or utilizing this knowledge. He decided that a good definition of freedom was complete external development without restraint of the personality. The self would simply develop into that which it was its nature to become. In other words, Schleiermacher was saying that freedom was the opportunity to develop one's potentialities without any type of interference.[29]

Since each nationality had different characteristics and traditions, it logically followed that freedom existed only in those countries where the national characteristics were allowed to develop in an uninhibited way. Those nationalities which developed their skills and innate talents without restraint would ultimately rise to a level where an obvious superiority would be recognized. After all, noted Schleiermacher, had this very thing not happened in Germany in the field of theology? When speaking about the nature of true religion there actually was no other satisfactory example of true religion except that of the German people. "To whom should I turn if not to the sons of Germany?" he asked. "Where else is there an audience for my speech?"[30] Schleiermacher assured his readers in *Speeches on Religion* that he did not boast about German spiritual insight because of some blind predilection for his native soil or because he spoke the German language, either of which was grounds enough for boasting by the average nationalist. He took an even more extreme nationalistic position by asserting that the Germans were the only people who were "capable, as well as worthy, of having awakened [in them] a sensitivity for holy and divine things."[31]

Having assumed such an ardently nationalistic position, he hastened to prove his point by comparing the people of the German states with Frenchmen and Englishmen. He maintained that it would be a waste of time to appeal to the English concerning matters of deep spirituality because they were too involved in gain and enjoyment. To them religion was a sham. As with their freedom, they put religion to the service of their selfish interests. They actually knew nothing of true religion, for they preached love and devotion for the Church in its historic form and ancient usages but they did so only from ulterior motives. They considered the Church and its traditions as a part of their constitution and as a means of protecting the state against its natural enemies.

Though the English lacked what the Germans possessed, they were

---

[29] Brandt, *Philosophy of Schleiermacher,* pp. 136–137.
[30] *Über die Religion* in Schleiermacher, *Sämmtliche Werke, Zur Theologie,* I, 153.
[31] *Ibid.,* I, 153.

in a much better situation than the wretched French. Compared to the
English the French were barbarians looking with indifference at the
historic events taking place in their land. Schleiermacher could not
believe that a nation of people so engrossed in destroying their traditions
as the French could be capable of deep religious feelings. Although he
did not say it in so many words he certainly indicated that a reverence
for God and a devotion to national traditions were synonymous. As a
final word of evidence against the spirituality of the French, Schleiermacher showed his attachment to laws based on tradition by asking,
"What does religion detest more than the unbridled arrogance with
which rulers of the people offer defiance to the traditional laws of the
world."[32]

Convinced that he had shown by comparison with Germans that
neither the French nor the English were worthy of matters which were
deeply spiritual, he turned once more with nationalistic fervor to the
subject of the superior nature of the German people and the more whole-
some religious atmosphere in the German states. With a nationalistic
faith that bordered on naïveté he said of Germany:

Only in my native land is there that happy climate which excludes nothing
entirely. There is found everything that beautifies nature, even though it may
only be scattered. At least in individual cases everything that develops attains
its most beautiful form. Neither wise moderation nor studious contemplation is
lacking; it is here therefore that religions must find a refuge from the coarse
barbarism and the cold worldly mind of the age.[33]

The fact that Schleiermacher was so full of praise for the religious
nature of the German people is a good indication that he would have
heaped as much praise on almost any other aspect of German life. Religion just happened to be the topic in this particular case. One must
also keep in mind that Schleiermacher was extremely vague about the
meaning of "Germany" and "native land." Several years were yet to
pass before he would be able to distinguish even for himself the political
implications of the term "Germany." He was thinking in terms of generalities where idealization was easy. Like many immature nationalists
he was willing to attribute to the "German people" superior qualities
which he would not admit existed in any particular German state or
group of people.

This nationalistic immaturity could be quite clearly seen in the way

[32] *Ibid.*, I, 153–154.
[33] *Ibid.*, I, 154.

in which Schleiermacher treated the subject of religion in a specific German state, Prussia. After having praised in a general way the superior religious environment of Germany, he had nothing but words of contempt for the Protestant Church of Prussia. When he looked at the total picture of religious life in Germany everything was wonderful. When he surveyed particular instances of this same religious life he could express nothing but dismay. He admitted that he could not blame the romanticists for criticizing what passed for religion in Prussia since he, too, felt that Prussian religious life was in a lamentable state. As he expressed it, "Your very contempt for the poverty-stricken and powerless venerators of religion, in whom, from lack of nourishment, religion perishes before it is born, convinces me that you have a bent toward religion."[34] He also made it clear to the romanticists that he shared their contempt for the leaders of German religious life, and, for that matter, for all the leaders of the various German states. In a statement that revealed both idealistic nationalism and realistic particularism he maintained that in spite of the rich cultural background of Germany, his homeland was "burdened with a very high degree of imperfection" and had demonstrated "small ability to prevent or abolish injustice."[35]

Schleiermacher's appraisal of religious conditions in Prussia as compared with his belief in the innate superiority of the German people illustrates the dilemma in which his nationalism placed him. He was exercising what Carlton J. H. Hayes referred to as nationalistic faith, which in simple terms was designated by Hayes as a faith in the destiny of a nation, a faith in what ought to be and not necessarily in what actually exists.[36] Yet, he was not completely dominated by this nationalistic faith, for his realistic nature forced him to admit that the particular instances of German society with which he came in contact in Prussia were certainly not to be greatly admired.

The deep conflicts resulting from the obvious contradiction between what Germany should be and what it actually was, caused Schleiermacher to lash out in anger against the invisible enemies of Germany who were preventing the natural progress of the German nation. He was exhibiting what has been called nationalistic intolerance[37] when he denounced the entire state system in Prussia by saying:

This is the extreme of utilitarianism to which the age with rapid strides is being hurried by worthless scholastic word-wisdom. This new barbarism is a fitting

[34] *Ibid.*, I, 252.
[35] *Ibid.*, I, 164.
[36] Carlton J. H. Hayes, *Nationalism: A Religion,* p. 165.
[37] *Ibid.*, p. 171.

opposite to the old one. It is the lovely result of the paternal eudiamonistic politics which has taken the place of the ruder despotism and which pervades every aspect of life.[38]

Schleiermacher was not more intolerant of what he saw in Prussia than of abuses elsewhere in Germany. He was just more aware of Prussia's political iniquities.

It is interesting to note that as an angry nationalist he used the same generalities in attacking the enemies of "Germany" as he had employed in defending the superiority of the "German people." Like many young nationalists who begin to make utterances against the enemies of their nation, he was not yet able to point with assurance toward any specific person or institution which personified the "enemy." This is understandable if one keeps in mind that in 1799, the year which he spent writing his *Speeches on Religion,* Schleiermacher was not too sure whether he was defending Prussia and a few other German states, all the German states, or just Prussia. Also, like many other young nationalists he had a tendency to attribute all of his "homeland's" problems to a single source. Like the African nationalist who decries the colonial system, the German nationalist who denounces Jews, or the American nationalist who assails communism, Schleiermacher tried to find one single source of difficulty which, if removed, would allow the natural flow of nationalistic spirit in Germany. He finally decided that the villain in Prussia as well as in most of the German states was the close relationship which existed between the Church and the state.

Since the German people were superior to other people because of their superior religious nature, and since the superior qualities of the German people had been rendered less effective than they should have been in developing a superior German nation, obviously every factor which hindered the work of the ecclesiastical institutions should be removed. If these institutions were as corrupt as Schleiermacher felt they were, then the corruptor was the state. By establishing a constitutional basis for the Church, with all the special privileges this involved, the state had delegated to that religious body many tasks which its members would not have performed under normal circumstances and which they were often not equipped to perform. These delegated responsibilities had

---

[38] *Über die Religion* in Schleiermacher, *Sämmtliche Werke, Zur Theologie,* I, 298.

in turn attracted to religious groups many people who were interested in the duties of the Church instead of their own spirituality.[39]

After having given to the Church constitutional privileges and official responsibilities the state had demanded that in return the religious bodies should express their gratitude by consciously serving the interests of the state.[40] Because the state had delegated civil duties to theologians the state also demanded the right to regulate their activities through which these civil duties were performed. Schleiermacher felt that the main result of this close relationship of the Church and the various German states was the subservience of the Church to the state, which meant that theologians had designed their religious program to meet the needs of the state. Baptism, burial, and marriage, having become merely civil functions carried on by ecclesiastical representatives, had lost both their religious significance and their spiritual value. The results of the servitude of the Church were that in "all its regulations there is nothing which pertains to religion alone, nor is there anything in which religion is the chief subject. In sacred lectures and directions, even in the most holy and sacred affairs, everything has a legal and civil connotation."[41]

Schleiermacher was not implying that the state should not rely upon and use the power of religious sentiment, for religious sentiment would naturally play a vital part in the life of any state inhabited by large numbers of Christians. He was opposed only to the manipulations of the religious feelings of the citizens in order to further the aims and goals of the state. He was finally convinced that the state should allow religious sentiment in Germany to make its natural course without guidance by the political authorities. In his determination to free religious life in Germany from state interference he was focusing attention upon a belief held by leading authorities on nationalism: that religious experience was closely akin to the spirit which motivated a group of people to have an awareness of national distinctives.[42] Consequently, any act which served to limit the free development of true spiritual religion would automatically curtail the growth of the national consciousness among the German people.

In the place of the existing relationship between Church and state Schleiermacher suggested an alternative which would strengthen the

[39] Ibid., I, 341.
[40] Ibid., I, 341–342.
[41] Ibid., I, 343.
[42] Hayes, Nationalism: A Religion, pp. 11–19, 164–182.

ability of both the state and the Church to stimulate national devotion among the German people. He proposed that the Church should surrender its traditional task of education in Germany to the state.[43] He could justify such a revolutionary departure from tradition because this was to him the only step which would help the Church maintain a proper spiritual nature and at the same time give the state a maximum opportunity for teaching patriotic devotion. Both the Church and the state would benefit if the state controlled public education but both would suffer irreparable damage if the changes in the educational system were not made quickly. If the state controlled education, then the Church could cease to be a servant of the state and return to the task of relating man to God.

For the first time in German history the state could properly assume the direct responsibility for controlling the total civic life of its citizens. Schleiermacher was perfectly frank in saying that it was time for the state to stop hiding behind the robes of the ecclesiastical institutions of Germany. If the state wished to see its citizens express loyalty and devotion, then the state and not the Church would have to instill that loyalty in them. According to Schleiermacher:

If the state requires a special discipline in order to produce certain responses among its citizens, this must not have to come from the Church. If there is a universal feeling of the necessity of it, then the state may rely upon families, but as elements of the civil and not as elements of the ecclesiastical society.[44]

In 1799 Schleiermacher was able to see what many modern nationalists discovered with regard to state control of education processes, or for that matter, of any means of communication: that political leaders could be sure of the nationalistic indoctrination of people only if the state itself directly controlled and supervised the transmission of these ideas. Whenever the state left the work of indoctrination to any organization the indoctrination would be diluted by the aims and views of that organization. In the case of the educational work of the ecclesiastical institutions of Germany, double damage was done to the process of instilling nationalism because the value of the Church as a bearer of German tradition was weakened by its duties to the state. This is why Schleiermacher's plea for the preservation of a purely spiritual Church in Germany was synonymous with a call for an increase in nationalistic efforts in German

---

[43] *Über die Religion* in Schleiermacher, *Sämmtliche Werke, Zur Theologie*, I, 379–381.
[44] *Ibid.*, I, 380.

states like Prussia. In hoping to safeguard both the biblical role of the Church and the educational role of the state, he summed up his feelings by demanding, "Away then with every such union between Church and state! That remains my Cato's utterance to the end, or until I see the union actually destroyed."[45]

Having stated his convictions in a way that would leave no possible room for misunderstanding, Schleiermacher then stepped completely out of character by conjuring up the specter of a revolutionary upheaval in Germany if the separation of Church and state was not soon realized. Almost threateningly he asked, "Will it be, as in nearby countries, only after a great commotion and a simultaneous movement everywhere? Will the state by a friendly arrangement terminate the unhappy marriage with the Church without the death and resurrection of both the state and the Church?"[46]

Publication of *Speeches on Religion* was a big step forward for Schleiermacher as far as his concept of national devotion was concerned. True, he was thinking in terms of vague generalities instead of concrete particulars but, nevertheless, he was moving toward a clearer vision of the personal responsibilities of citizens to their linguistic group. At the same time he was realizing the importance of tradition and custom as well as the need for recognition of linguistic ties; he was also making halting movements to defend those unique characteristics that set off the German people from other nationalities. He had not yet reached the level where he could intelligently ask himself the central question confronting the nationalist: "What actually is this nationalism which is now so universal?"[47] He was not yet even aware that he felt a close affection for his German language and for the ties created by it; but neither was he able to identify this feeling with any emotion with which he was familiar.

Quite naturally Schleiermacher's quickening nationalism was expressed in other publications. A number of documents dated about the same time as the *Speeches on Religion* reveal the same spirit, although none of them were as lengthy or as comprehensive as his first book. These documents, while not relating directly to nationalism or to nationalistic topics, demonstrate the intensity of concern he exhibited for his king and for Prussia and his corresponding search for a better relationship between the German people and their leaders. One such document was a sermon which he preached in Potsdam before Friedrich Wilhelm III at

[45] *Ibid.*, I, 350.
[46] *Ibid.*
[47] Hayes, *Nationalism: A Religion,* p. 2.

the Royal Garrison Church in March, 1799. In this sermon he told his listeners that they should take note of the fact that Christ lived on this earth for the single purpose of some day dying for the sake of man's righteousness. This was the only way for Christ to fulfill His responsibility to man. There was nothing unusual about Schleiermacher's point of emphasis, for probably half of the sermons preached by evangelical ministers has this as their theme. The nationalistic significance of the sermon was in the application of the principle of living with a definite purpose. He pointed out to the King and his court that it was not necessary for men in places of earthly responsibility to be taken from their tasks in order to give meaning and value to their lives. On the contrary, few men had as good an opportunity to serve their country and bring honor to themselves as did the servants of the state. If Prussia's leadership ever reached the place where the king and his assistants could no longer reform abuses and introduce improvements, then truly a day of grief would come upon the country.[48]

Schleiermacher was trying to show Friedrich Wilhelm III that as king of Prussia he must recognize that he had been given a trust. The nation was an organic whole, of which the king was only one part. If he did not fulfill his obligations to the people who were a nation, not just his subjects, then of course the nation would suffer and the king would be dishonored.

A second document showing Schleiermacher's awakening nationalism was a letter which he wrote late in 1799 to a friend concerning the death of an obscure civil servant. In this letter Schleiermacher went to great lengths in criticizing the Prussian government for allowing advancement on the basis of friendship or political connections instead of on the basis of competence. The recent death of a very capable civil servant had made a strong impression upon him because he knew that with so much incompetence in public office the death of a dedicated public official was a loss to the nation.[49] Even as early as 1799 he was thinking in terms of gain and loss for the nation. Although he did not discuss the idea of death for the sake of the nation until 1806, he quite obviously was prepared to make some extreme demands upon the citizens for the nation.

It is difficult to consider Schleiermacher's *Speeches on Religion* and

---

[48] "Einige Empfindungen des sterbenden Jesus, wie auch wir uns für unsere letzten Augenblicke wünschen sollen," in Schleiermacher, *Sämmtliche Werke, Predigten, I,* 41–53.

[49] Schleiermacher to Charlotte von Kathen from Berlin, December 2, 1799, Reimer (ed.), *Aus Schleiermachers Leben,* I, 235–237.

the other contemporary documents relating to his nationalism without taking into account the *Soliloquies,* written and published one year after the *Speeches on Religion.* Both of these major works were intended to supply answers to questions raised by a specific group of people. The first had been intended for the romanticists, while the second was intended for critics of *Speeches on Religion.* The *Soliloquies* was thus only a continuation of the nationalistic exploration which Schleiermacher had begun in his first book.

He began the *Soliloquies* with an inquiry into the nature of freedom. Once he had caught a vision of the nature of individual freedom, he was able to expand the concept to encompass the nation. He came to see that the same factors which would contribute to the happiness and fulfillment of the free individual would also increase the happiness of a nation of individuals. It seems at first glance that in his *Soliloquies* Schleiermacher approached nationalism in a backward or at least peculiar way. This may be true, but the fact remains that once he clearly saw the individual as capable of freeing himself by recognizing his unique characteristics and values, it was but a short step to the application of this principle to the German nation, which he viewed as an organism or "person."

Schleiermacher told his readers in the opening sentence of the *Soliloquies* that the greatest gift he could give to them would be the example of the spirit's "intimate conversation with itself. For this is the greatest achievement there is, a clear and undisturbed view of the free personality."[50] With "free" man as his announced goal, he unfolded his thoughts in five impressive and very beautifully arranged meditations.

The first meditation was of little importance as far as nationalistic content is concerned for in it Schleiermacher merely chided the slave of circumstances who lived his life by adjusting to his environment. The second and third meditations were more important, for in them he waged a polemic against Kant and Fichte by magnifying the role of the conscience and showing its unque influence upon one's individualism. Focusing attention upon the Ego, the individual, the free personality capable of creation and destruction by its own will, Schleiermacher maintained that the inner man was the point of origin of all freedom because only "his innermost activity, the place where his true nature abides, is free, and in contemplating it, I feel myself to be at the sacred foundation of freedom, far from all debasing limitation."[51] Following

[50] Friedrich Schleiermacher, *Werke Schleiermachers,* p. 176.
[51] *Ibid.,* pp. 180–181.

this logic to its conclusion, Schleiermacher asserted that no man could ever know any kind of freedom until he had set the "self" free.

Once into the concept of individual freedom he could talk of nothing else. The fourth and fifth meditations, in which he spoke of mankind's destiny and the beautiful rhapsody of spiritual life, were only extensions of his original notion of freedom. They were the critical chapters of his work, however, as well as vital elements in his evolutionary development toward nationalism, for it was in these chapters that he expressed concern that man could be content with mere shadows of freedom. According to him man can never become free by arriving at some philosophical position that is founded on a universal concept; nor can he become free by submitting his life to the duties of the Church or the state. These activities do not raise man's level of activity high enough for him to realize the unique nature of freedom. Furthermore, freedom would never be gained by viewing the rough, shapeless masses of mankind that are supposedly alike but which are in a process of external transition.[52] But if freedom could not be gained in the traditional ways, that is to say, through philosophical speculation or service to mankind, how then was freedom to come to the heart of a man? With a simplicity that defies an immediate understanding and with a nationalistic impact that revolutionized Schleiermacher's own life just a few years later, he said that freedom was the act of beholding humanity within oneself, for this vision was seen by him to be the intimate and necessary tie between morality and theory.[53]

This realization furnished Schleiermacher the key for unlocking the mystery of nationalism because it was on this basis that he, a Prussian particularist, would be able to understand that in his own personality each Prussian must be able to see all of Prussia—its traditions, language, customs, laws, religion, and people. Later, when his nationalism matured and he applied this principle to Germany during the dark years before the War of Liberation, he came to understand that Germany could never rise above its limitations unless it looked upon itself as a nation. The same process which would lead to freedom for the individual would make a nation free. But if it was true that the factors causing personal freedom would also induce national freedom, it was also true that the inhibitions limiting the growth of personal freedom would stunt the growth of national freedom.

When Schleiermacher surveyed the political and intellectual scene in

[52] *Ibid.*, pp. 189–190.
[53] *Ibid.*, p. 187.

Germany he knew that the signs all pointed to a lack of the ingredients necessary for national consciousness. The Enlightenment had made the task of achieving nationalism almost impossible by masking decay with a false front of progress. In his heart Schleiermacher was confessing that for many years Germany would not know the freedom of which he spoke when he said in the *Soliloquies*: "Every last moment is supposed to have been full of progress. Oh, how much I despise this generation, which adorns itself more shamelessly than any other ever did."[54] This statement was one of the first indications that he grasped both the advantages and difficulties inherent in a nationalistic movement. He had a halting notion of what it would take to "free" the German people, but at the same time he could see that there was no immediate indication that the people of Germany would even want to be "free."

Here then was the young nationalist advancing an idealistic program which had no immediate possibility of succeeding. Unintentionally venturing beyond the subject of religion in his *Speeches on Religion* and *Soliloquies,* he stated principles concerning freedom and individual responsibility which were fundamentals for a nationalistic point of view. Scorning his homeland for its old-fashioned government and exalting the traditions of the German people, he called for a national interest in education and complete separation of the affairs of Church and state. He saw that the greatest problem facing Germany was the inertia which neutralized the natural superiority of the German way of life.[55] Most important of all for the growth of his understanding of nationalism, Schleiermacher by 1800 had arrived at the conviction that man can alter the course of history only by an act of his own will. This led him to pose for his own mind the question of whether the principle that he had discovered for the individual also held true for the nation. If so, then he was also faced with the problem of arousing the German people to exercise their will power in order to change the course of German history. He was not sure of the questions, let alone the answers, but of one fact he was more than sure: any act that helped either him or the German people to realize a greater degree of freedom would be worth whatever cost might be involved. Come what might, Schleiermacher could confidently declare, "My will rules fate, so long as I combine everything into this comprehensive aim, and remain indifferent with reference to external situations."[56]

---

54 *Ibid.,* p. 199–200.
55 *Ibid.,* pp. 212–213.
56 *Ibid.,* pp. 211–212.

Six years were to pass before he was to have the opportunity to test his theory on himself and on Germany. He was not a German nationalist in the full sense of the word in 1800, for he still did not have a clear understanding of the difference between his loyalty to Prussia and his obligation to Germany. Still, he had within him the feelings, emotions, and loyalties which would blossom as national patriotism as soon as a moment of crisis arrived.

One of the most difficult obstacles to overcome in studying nationalism is to arrive at a clear and precise definition of the terms involved. Expressions like "national consciousness," "national pride," and "cultural unity" are used to describe nationalism but these terms are hard to define because they deal with emotions, and thus are intangible. The ideal way to study nationalism would be to delve into the emotional life of a nationalist to see why he feels a devotion for a specific nationality, or why he senses superiority in his native culture. Since this type of investigation is impossible, the best alternative is to study the feelings of the nationalist as they were recorded in his letters, memoirs, journals, and other personal data. Only such an intimate acquaintance as that which results from a thorough search of private documents will answer the question of why a man became a nationalist.

In the case of Friedrich Schleiermacher the researcher is more fortunate than with most nationalists, for the young Berlin theologian left an extensive and intimate personal record of himself between 1800 and 1806—a record which goes far in explaining how he became increasingly aware of his own growth as a nationalist. While none of the many letters and sermons from his life during these six years reveals a precise moment when he discovered the basic principles of nationalism, they do show collectively that his personality was being subtly prepared for the day when he was to grasp the concept of nationalism as the only hope of salvation from the political chaos of Germany. By studying his life closely from 1800 until 1806, one can see that many of the changes brought about in his life, which made him move closer to the nationalistic viewpoint he assumed after 1806, were the result of the fortuitous unfolding of time and circumstances. The profound shock which he experienced in 1806 over the annihilation of the Prussian armies was an experience which he might never have known had the war been fought a decade, or even five years, earlier. His determination to rally Prussians to build a new nation on the ashes of the old one destroyed by Napoleon might have been completely out of character for him several years earlier. Such reactions were not spontaneous responses, but were conditioned by the events of Schleiermacher's life up to that time.

Because of the crucial nature of the period between 1800 and 1806, three interrelated developments in Schleiermacher's life should be scrutinized to reveal the diversity of the forces which molded his nationalistic point of view. First, the changes brought about in his life as a result of the publication of his *Speeches on Religion* and the *Soliloquies* were instrumental in preparing him for a greater capacity for nationalistic expression. Secondly, the reaction of the romanticists, for whose benefit the *Speeches on Religion* had been written, turned him away from the romantic circle and toward an independence of thought, without which he might never have progressed past the immature nationalism he had expressed by 1800. Thirdly, the reaction to his publications by his ecclesiastical superiors was significant for the growth of his nationalism because in trying to rescue him from the "depravity" of the romanticists they set in motion a chain of circumstances which resulted in his being at Halle at the time of the humiliation of the Prussian armies in 1806. While none of these developments "made" him a nationalist, each was instrumental in shaping his character and his disposition so that he ultimately came to see nationalism as the only hope for the German people.

The immediate result of the publication of his two major literary works was the psychological change that they made in Schleiermacher. If one needs a word to express the young author's attitude in 1800, that word would be "self-assurance," for with the writing of the *Speeches on Religion* and the *Soliloquies* the old fear of criticism, which had haunted him for many years, no longer was a problem. In fact, the very criticism he had feared while writing the *Speeches on Religion* became a source of amusement to him.[1] Sensing for the first time in his life that he had something valuable and worthwhile to say, and realizing that his contemporaries would listen to him, he felt a surge of confidence in himself and in his abilities.[2] His sense of dependence upon the romanticists slowly receded, to be replaced by what might be called cockiness. It was not that he felt superior to the romanticists; he just no longer felt that he needed

[1] Schleiermacher to Ehrenfried von Willich from Berlin, June 11, 1801, Heinrich Meisner (ed.), *Schleiermacher als Mensch: Sein Werden und Wirken, Familien-und Freundesbriefe*, I, 214–215.

[2] Friedrich Schelling to Wilhelm Schlegel from Berlin, June, 1801, Joseph Korner (ed.), *Briefe von und an August Wilhelm Schlegel*, II, 125.

them to express his thoughts for him. It was as though he had broken a psychological barrier which, at least until 1798, had made him fearful of independent scholarship. Gone was the natural tendency to hold back his ideas in a protective type of seclusion—a seclusion which would probably have prevented any significant work on controversial subjects. Now, for the first time Schleiermacher felt a genuine sense of achievement and satisfaction about something he had done. Of course, there is no way to estimate what he might or might not have done in the general area of nationalistic journalism if he had not received so much attention from his critics, the romanticists, and his ecclesiastical superiors. The point is that in the wake of the attention he received because of the publication of his *Speeches on Religion* and the *Soliloquies* he began the most prodigious and, as far as the development of his nationalism was concerned, the most important journalistic undertaking of his life: the translation and publication of the works of Plato. With a bolstered ego which was entirely out of character for him he spent the latter half of 1800 and all of 1801 on this monumental task, which he was never to finish.[3] His translation of Plato was significant in the development of his nationalistic point of view because he appropriated Plato's organistic concept of the state and used it as the foundation for his proposals for a unified German nation.

Partly as a result of his newly discovered feeling of independence and partly as an outgrowth of an awareness on his part that he no longer "needed" the romanticists, Schleiermacher slowly broke his ties with the activities of the Berlin group. With their help he had experienced what Koppel Pinson described as the evolution of the romanticist. According to Pinson, romanticism "was easily concerted from extreme individualism to the worship of the organic community and from the extolling of free personality to the recognition that true individuality is found only in the collective national individuality."[4] Schleiermacher had taken the path outlined by Pinson, and, having done so, was ready to sever his connections with the romanticists. He was naturally very grateful for the help and guidance which they had proffered him during the five years he had

[3] Schleiermacher to Henrietta Herz from Stolpe, August 10, 1802, Georg Reimer (ed.), *Aus Schleiermachers Leben in Briefen*, I, 312; Schleiermacher to Ehrenfried von Willich from Berlin, December 13, 1801, *ibid.*, I, 285–286; Schleiermacher to Eleanor Grünow, from Stolpe, July 19, 1802, *ibid.*, I, 306–309; Wilhelm Dilthey, *Leben Schleiermacher*, pp. 652–653.

[4] Koppel Pinson, *Modern Germany: Its History and Civilization*, p. 43; see also Theobold Ziegler, *Die geistigen und sozialen Strömungen des neunzehnten Jahrhunderts*, pp. 27–45.

spent in their company. However great his feeling of indebtedness might have been, and however strongly attached he might have felt to this group of intellectuals who had encouraged him to express himself openly, Schleiermacher, nevertheless, was not blind to the fact that he had never really felt himself to be a part of their circle. The differences of opinion between Friedrich and the romanticists had been the motivating factor leading him to write the *Speeches on Religion,* and he received no tangible evidence that his arguments for a better understanding of religion had any effect upon them. It should thus have been a surprise to no one that the young preacher decided to terminate their relationship. The significance of his decision to break with the romanticists lies in the fact that in turning away from them he moved closer to the nationalistic position he was to assume after the French attacked Prussia in 1806.

Although the particular circumstances may seem irrelevant on the surface, three different aspects of the rupture of relations between Schleiermacher and the romanticists played a major part in his further development as a nationalist. The first of these three rather intangible circumstances had to do with the matter of historical research. One historian has stated, "It is to the everlasting credit of the romantic movement to have brought about the deepening of the historical sense and the resulting development of scientific history."[5] Having had an unusual interest in historical research and especially in ancient Greek and Roman history since his days as a student at Barby, Schleiermacher recognized in the romanticists a corresponding sense of keen historical interest when he first came in contact with them in 1797. Probably no other romanticist influence upon him was as profound and far-reaching as was this sharp interest in studies of antiquity. Yet when he decided to put his interest in history to good use by translating Plato's Greek manuscripts into German texts, he experienced a deep disappointment. The romanticists were interested but would not cooperate.

Friedrich Schlegel, who was supposed to help him get the translations published, was so unreliable and inconsistent that Schleiermacher finally admitted to himself that he should never have consented to let Schlegel help him.[6] The impact of this experience on Schleiermacher was to alter not only his relationship with the romanticists but also the direction of his journalistic efforts for the rest of his life. In failing to pursue the

[5] Pinson, *Modern Germany,* p. 45.
[6] Schleiermacher to Henrietta Herz from Stolpe, August 10, 1802, Reimer (ed.), *Aus Schleiermachers Leben,* I, 312–313; Dilthey, *Leben Schleiermachers,* pp. 652–686.

practical objectives which were within reach, the romanticists had demonstrated quite forcibly to their theological associate that they were basically an impractical group. Schleiermacher realized that they had good ideas on culture, language, traditions, and individualism, but he felt that they had too difficult a time translating their ideas into common experiences of life. To him, if ideas had no practical application they were useless.

A second aspect of Schleiermachers' termination of personal associations with the romanticists which furthered his nationalistic development was his concern over their lack of social propriety. Time and again he experienced personal embarrassment or humiliation because of the inability of his fellow romanticists to make the transition from a world of ideals to a world of people and facts. The classic example of this type of experience was the embarrassment which came to him because of the infamous scandal over Friedrich Schlegel's romance with Dorothea Veit. Like most of the romanticists, Schlegel made a cult of estheticism, looking at human existence as though it were art. This principle worked well until Schlegel applied this carefree principle to his personal relationship with a married woman in Berlin. The results were not very poetic. The scandal which resulted from the illicit affair involved not only Schlegel but the entire romantic circle, for each of the romanticists felt obligated to defend Schlegel from the criticisms of Berlin society. The whole affair put Schleiermacher in an awkward position, for he had also become involved with a married woman by the name of Eleanor Grünow. Neither Friedrich nor Eleanor looked upon their relationship as illicit or unclean, and actually the two were guilty of nothing more serious than contemplating a divorce for Eleanor from her husband. Since he and Eleanor had conducted their personal affairs with circumspection and propriety, he could not understand why Schlegel could not have been as respectful of public sentiment. To make matters even worse, in defending Schlegel from the abuse of the critics Schleiermacher seemed to be defending his own love affair with Eleanor. Consequently, by defending Schlegel he drew to himself almost as much abuse and ill treatment as Schlegel was receiving.[7]

As a result of this whole sordid affair Schleiermacher became convinced that social respect was a fundamental necessity, even for one who wished to revolutionize his society. Having briefly experienced the exclusion which society exercises against one who has broken the rules of

[7] Schleiermacher to Charlotte Schleiermacher from Berlin, July 1, 1801, Reimer (ed.), *Aus Schleiermachers Leben,* I, 270–274.

proper conduct, he never again evinced any desire to stand against the
current of tradition. In a very practical way he learned the fundamental
law of the nationalist: tradition is a matter of culture and as such is the
basis of nationality.[8]

From that time on he was more concerned than ever before with tradition and with the preservation of an unbroken sequence of historical
events in Germany, seeing that Germany, like an individual in society,
could not progress from lesser to greater degrees of happiness and at the
same time violate the dictates of tradition. He may have wavered on
other elements of his nationalism in later years, but after the Schlegel
scandal he never compromised on his belief that the only progress possible for any group of people was the progress made as a conscious effort
at moving from a lower to a higher form of national development.

The third aspect of Schleiermacher's break with the romanticists had
to do with the beginning of a prolonged personal feud between Friedrich
and the most recent addition to the romantic circle in Berlin, Johann
Gottlieb Fichte. This feud not only signaled the end of his associations
with the Berlin group, it also was instrumental in stimulating his thoughts
along the line of nationalistic development. From the time when the
two men were introduced in 1799[9] until Fichte's death in 1814, they saw
almost everything in life from opposite points of view; yet they were so
deeply interested in the same subjects that they were constantly thrown
together. Since Schleiermacher spent a great deal of his energies for a
number of years in criticizing Fichte's writings, which were as nationalistic as Schleiermacher's writings, if not more so, it must be said that
Fichte was greatly responsible for the clarification of Schleiermacher's
nationalistic thinking after 1800.

In order to understand exactly how Fichte caused his protagonist to
clarify his position with reference to nationalism, it is necessary to understand the views of the two men on the problem of freedom of action for
the individual within any segment of society. Fichte thought in terms of
Kantian freedom for the individual, which meant that he wanted to
mold the individual to fit the group. In one sense of the word Fichte was
more "nationalistic" than Schleiermacher because Fichte was thinking
in terms of the German nation while Schleiermacher was still thinking in
terms of freedom for individual Germans, with little or no reference to
the possibility of a national German state. However, by 1800 Fichte was
not yet at the place where he could understand the role of such a creation

[8] Carlton J. H. Hayes, *Nationalism: A Religion*, pp. 4–5.
[9] Johann G. Fichte, *Fichtes Leben und literarischer Briefwechsel*, I, 313–314.

as a German national state, for he was thinking in terms of cosmopolitanism. He was more concerned with the role of Germany in international affairs than he was with the creation and development of a unique and complete German fatherland.[10]

Having already discarded Kantian ethics and having rejected Kant's idea of the submergence of the individual will to the categorical will of society, Schleiermacher felt that Fichte was placing the accent at the wrong place. The young Berlin theologian insisted that Fichte must be wrong in neglecting the right to exercise individualism,[11] and it was while he was stoutly opposing Fichte that Schleiermacher began to see that a nation was a collection of individuals who were exercising their individuality but whose natures were so much alike that there was harmony among the individuals. He was beginning to see that individuals could be free and still have similarities which welded them into national units. This seems a logical conclusion to what he had said earlier in the *Soliloquies,* and it is quite possible that Schleiermacher would have come to the same conclusions without Fichte's help. Nevertheless, Schleiermacher was obviously blending Fichte's idea on submergence of the individual will to the will of the group with his own concept of individualism within the social structure. Compelled by a growing dislike for the Berlin philosopher[12] he moved closer and closer to an unreserved declaration that a nation of individuals with similar cultural backgrounds afforded the only real hope for the expression of true individualism.

To see the full effect of Schleiermacher's opposition to Fichte and to understand the way Schleiermacher began to talk himself into a more apparent nationalistic position, one should consider two letters by Schleiermacher. One of them was written to a friend in 1803, the other was a more formal letter to Friedrich Schlegel in 1804. Both of the letters show that he had undergone a tremendous change in his attitude about Ger-

---

[10] Helmuth Engelbrecht, *Johann Gottlieb Fichte,* p. 82; "Der Patriotismus und sein Gegentheil," in Johann G. Fichte, *Johann Gottlieb Fichtes nachgelassene Werke,* III, 225–228; Eugene N. Anderson, *Nationalism and the Cultural Crisis in Prussia,* pp. 25–26, 35; Richard Brandt, *The Philosophy of Schleiermacher,* pp. 42–53.

[11] "Grundlinien einer Kritik der bisherigen Sittenlehre," in Friedrich Schleiermacher, *Sämmtliche Werke, Zur Philosophie,* I, 1–344; Brandt, *Philosophy of Schleiermacher,* pp. 166–175.

[12] Schleiermacher to Ehrenfried von Willich from Berlin, June 11, 1801, Reimer (ed.), *Aus Schleiermachers Leben,* I, 278–281; Schleiermacher to Henrietta Herz from Stolpe, September 16, 1802, *ibid.,* I, 337–338; Schleiermacher to Henrietta Herz from Stolpe, June 10, 1803, *ibid.,* I, 366–367; Schleiermacher to Ehrenfried von Willich from Stolpe, January 28, 1804, *ibid.,* I, 389–391.

many and German ways since his pessimistic statements in *Speeches on Religion*. Like the nationalist Herder,[13] Schleiermacher began to ignore the Slavs of German character and to accentuate the superior qualities of his homeland. In fact, in expressing what amounted to chauvinistic pride in Germany, he indicated that his own sense of reason was giving way to emotionalism, thus removing the last important barrier to a serious nationalistic faith. Nationalism has never been a matter to be submitted to logical processes or to analytical investigation by its adherents,[14] and one of Schleiermacher's difficulties with the patriotic feelings he felt for Germany had been his various attempts to understand his feelings in logical terms. These letters, written in 1803 and 1804, indicate that he no longer was worried with rationalizing his feelings, being willing instead to state freely his pride in Germany without feeling a compulsion to prove what he was saying.

In the first of the two letters Schleiermacher directed his attention to a comparison of French and German tragic novels. He had just finished reading a French novel and assured Henrietta Herz, the friend to whom he wrote the letter, that the book had bolstered his belief that German culture was superior to French culture. He said that French tragedies were decidedly inferior because the French based their works on the moral principles of Frenchmen, and since the moral level of the French people was low, writings based on these morals would also be of a lowly character. With contempt for Frenchmen and feelings of pride for the German people, he declared that a German could not help regarding the literary products of France with scorn. Obviously Schleiermacher was making an appeal for the recognition of German superiority on the basis of pure emotionalism, with no thought that he was possibly guilty of using a faulty chain of logic. Even more significantly, Schleiermacher added that as far as he was concerned the only good French books were those which were permeated with nationalism. This was the first time perhaps that he had expressed so boldly his belief that only nationalistic journalism, even the French variety, was worthy of praise.[15]

Schleiermacher's growing dependence upon emotionalism as proof for nationalistic beliefs became apparent in a letter written to Friedrich Schlegel in 1804. For some time the two had carried on an extensive cor-

[13] Carlton J. H. Hayes, "Contributions of Herder to the Doctrine of Nationalism," *American Historical Review*, xxxii, No. 4, (July, 1927), 730–731.

[14] Salo W. Baron, *Modern Nationalism and Religion*, pp. 3–6; Hans Kohn, *Nationalism: Its Meaning and History*, p. 9.

[15] Schleiermacher to Henrietta Herz from Stolpe, July 30, 1803, Reimer (ed.), *Aus Schleiermachers Leben*, I, 373–374.

respondence concerning the philosophical implications of works by Fichte and the other romanticists, and the matter of the value of German philosophers had entered into the discussions. In what must be regarded as the most chauvinistic and blindly nationalistic statement Schleiermacher had ever made, he told Schlegel that neither the English nor the French were capable of becoming scholars in traditional philosophy. According to him only the Germans possessed that fine sense of continuity necessary to connect the past with the present. In his opinion, only Germans could produce a valuable interpretation of world events, because only Germans were capable of building great philosophical systems on the basis of investigation into the works of the great scholars of the past.[16]

These nationalistic outbursts on subjects like the superiority of German novels or the superiority of German philosophers were symptomatic of the changes which had taken place in Schleiermacher's thinking after 1800. In part reflecting the long series of events dating back to his youth, which were just beginning to take on shape and meaning in the form of nationalism, these chauvinistic utterances also mirrored the more immediate influences of his departure from the romantic circle and his growth in self-confidence. Still, the expressions of nationalistic pride exhibited by him in private letters did not mean that nationalism was the unifying factor in his outlook upon life. Being no more certain of nationalism as a solution to the problems of society than he had been of Pietism, rationalism, or romanticism, he was more or less fencing with nationalism to find its weaknesses and strengths. Before he could arrive at the place where nationalism would be the most dynamic force in his life, Shleiermacher would first have to undergo an experience which would destroy all the secondary allegiances which had occupied his attention for so many years. He had gone as far as he could on his own toward being a nationalist. The final step would come only when he would be driven to choose nationalism as a complete and total answer to all problems faced by his society, or by any other; only a cataclysmic event would have the force to push him past the indistinguishable line which separates the nationalist from the average citizen. The war between France and Prussia in 1806, with the resulting collapse of the Prussian armies and the humiliating peace terms dictated to Prussia by Napoleon, proved to be the final factor needed to turn him to nationalism with a complete and almost reckless abandon.

[16] Schleiermacher to Friedrich Schlegel from Stolpe, May 26, 1804, Meisner (ed.), *Schleiermacher als Mensch*, I, 343.

By an unusual turn of events, between 1800 and 1806 Schleiermacher was teaching at the University of Halle when the war with the French began, and this vantage point let him see the collapse of Prussian morale as well as the collapse of the military formations. The story of how he came to be at Halle to witness the complete depravity of Prussia begins with the publication of the *Soliloquies,* and this unique chain of events probably played as much a part in causing Schleiermacher to espouse nationalism as did any of the many other influences on his life.

Schleiermacher's theological "deviations" in his *Speeches on Religion* and in his *Soliloquies* convinced his ecclesiastical superiors of the Reformed Church that the romanticists were exercising a harmful influence on their young chaplain. To remedy what they considered merely a matter of poor environment they had him transferred to a small church at Stolpe.

It soon became obvious that much more was involved in his criticism of Church affairs than just unhealthy surroundings. One would quite naturally have expected Schleiermacher as a minister of the Gospel to take the theological position that the Church, the earthly representation of God's grace, constituted the hope of mankind. He would have been an unusual minister if he had had no faith in ecclesiastical institutions as a transforming factor in society even though he seriously questioned many of their orthodox doctrines. He reflected his faith in the social effectiveness of religious institutions in his *Speeches on Religion* when he pleaded for a separation of civil and ecclesiastical affairs on the basis of a belief that the Church could never fulfill its civil responsibilities and still remain a guide in spiritual matters. At the same time, the major portion of his criticism of religious institutions was directed toward the loss of their effectiveness because of the close Church-state relationship in Prussia. Thus, if the purpose for sending Schleiermacher to Stolpe was to turn his thoughts away from criticism and toward a more intensive pastoral concern, the two years he spent in Stolpe were wasted time. Finding more time for study than ever before once he was away from the busy social life of Berlin, and realizing a new feeling of freedom since he was no longer closely associated with the romanticists, he began in earnest the pursuit of the elusive shadow of nationalism involved in the question of the Church-state relationship in Prussia. In other words, the transfer of Schleiermacher to Stolpe served only to stimulate his desire to clarify for himself the exact status of the Church and, coincidentally, the exact nature of the state. He was on the verge of asking himself the most fundamental question that a nationalist can ask, "What is the state?"

The first noticeable result of Schleiermacher's attempts to determine the exact nature of the Church with relationship to the state following his move to Stolpe was a lengthy and very scholarly pamphlet entitled, "Two Impartial Judgments on Protestant Ecclesiastical Affairs," which he wrote in 1803.[17] As the title suggests, he concentrated on the question of the continued separation of the Lutheran and Reformed confessions in Prussia, but he kept turning to the larger question of the value of one church for Prussia as opposed to two church bodies as they existed in 1803. Intending to discuss only the structure of the Reformed and Lutheran faiths and their relative value to Prussia, he instead ended up discussing the position of the state and the part that the state played in the operations of the Church. More and more he found that he was unable to discuss religious affairs as though they were isolated factors of society. Aside from the numerous letters and short references exhibiting nationalistic inclinations, already cited in previous chapters, this pamphlet contains Schleiermacher's first serious efforts at defining the responsibility to the government by an institution like the Church.

The basic thesis underlying the arguments of his pamphlet is that neither of the two Protestant confessions in Prussia could properly function as a separate religious body, and thus neither could fulfill its obligations as an institution to God or to the state. The holy obligation of the Church, the task of relating the lost to the grace of God, would never be realized simply because of the division of the bride of Christ into opposing factions. But of even greater significance for Schleiermacher's nationalism was his feeling that if the Church did not fulfill its obligations to society the state would suffer because of the lack of spiritual understanding among its citizens. In other words, the Church did not exist just for the benefit of the work of the Gospel; it also existed to serve the needs of the state.[18] He was not indicating that he thought religious bodies should be a tool in the hands of the state government and be controlled by the government of Prussia. Far from it. As he had already made quite clear in his *Speeches on Religion,* the Church could never be a true spiritual guide as long as it was dominated by the state. What he was ad-

---

[17] "Zwei unvorgreifliche Gutachten in Sachen des protestantischen Kirchenwesens zunächst in Beziehung auf den Preussischen Staat," in Schleiermacher, *Sämmtliche Werke, Zur Theologie,* V, 41–156.

[18] *Ibid.,* V, 46–49, 50–67, 74–93.

vocating in "Two Impartial Judgments on Protestant Ecclesiastical Affairs" was the realization by the Church of its obligation to serve the needs of the state. Grasping the principle that even holy institutions like the Church "owed" the state certain specified results in the lives of its communicants was a cardinal step in his evolutionary progress as a nationalist. Of course, in 1803 he was still thinking in terms of a relationship between the churches of Prussia and the Prussian states—a restricted point of view, which would persist until he rose above his particularism in the War of Liberation—but the key argument which he made in the pamphlet was the principle of complete authority of the state and, later, of the nation.

About the same time that Schleiermacher wrote "Two Impartial Judgments on Protestant Ecclesiastical Affairs" his career, as well as his development as a nationalist, took an unusual turn when he was offered a position as professor of Practical Theology at the University of Würzburg in Bavaria. Having been in financial difficulties for a number of years, he was tempted to look upon the security of a professor's salary as a relief from near-poverty. On the other hand, he could see several good reasons for not taking the position. Friedrich Schelling taught at Würzburg, and Schleiermacher was not sure that he could work under a domineering personality like Schelling's. Then, too, Schleiermacher had been plagued for a number of years with a stomach disorder and was afraid that the summer climate of Würzburg might accentuate his physical difficulties. The final persuasion that decided him against the appointment was the advice given to him by Johann Joachim Spalding, a noted Prussian theologian and philosopher. He told Schleiermacher to be patient, for Prussia would have need of his services and he would thus be doing his state a great disservice by leaving.[19] Schleiermacher did not know that, along with a number of other people, Spalding was working to secure an appointment for him at the University of Halle. When his appointment was announced in 1804 Schleiermacher still did not know that Spalding had been instrumental in securing the position at Halle, believing instead that Karl von Beyme, a Prussian privy councillor, had read his pamphlet on the ecclesiastical problem and had been so impressed that he appointed Schleiermacher to the state teaching position.[20]

---

[19] Dilthey, *Leben Schleiermachers,* pp. 699–710.
[20] Schleiermacher to Henrietta Herz from Stolpe, April, 1804, Reimer (ed.), *Aus Schleiermachers Leben,* I, 394–395; Schleiermacher to Ehrenfried von Willich from Stolpe, May 21, 1804, *ibid.,* I, 395; Dilthey, *Leben Schleiermachers,* pp. 641–643.

Schleiermacher's immediate response to what he considered a sign of favor by the Prussian government indicated that although he had progressed in his nationalistic development he still did not possess any clear understanding of the difference between loyalty to Germany and service to Prussia. This inability to distinguish between particularist interests and nationalism was especially obvious in a letter which he wrote to a friend soon after he had received notification of his Halle appointment. He stated that he was pleased beyond description by the chance to remain in the "fatherland" where things were well-ordered and where traditions dated back to ancient times. The people of Prussia were his people and the laws by which Prussia was governed were the laws which he understood and loved. Most significantly, he stated that Prussian laws and the entire system which these laws supported would give him the most pleasant life he could ever want.[21] It is true that he could have been speaking in broad generalities and that what he said could have been applied equally well to Germany or Prussia, but the evidence seems to indicate that he was simply applying nationalistic principles within a particularistic frame of reference. He could talk about Germany and make references to the German language or customs, but he still was thinking in terms of specific geographic entities. If one took him literally Schleiermacher was saying that he would be satisfied with no other political structure than the one in which Prussia existed as a state, separated from and uninfluenced by other German states. This is only one more indication that he had progressed in his nationalistic growth to the point where only a dramatic event would force him to clarify his ideas about allegiance to state and nationality.

Upon arriving at Halle in 1804 for his new position as lecturer for the University and preacher at the University Church, Schleiermacher seemingly put away his thoughts on nationalism. The calm serenity of Halle, the economic security of his position, and the close friendships he soon established all helped him to arrive at a peace of mind which he had never before known. For the next two years he wrote virtually nothing of significance concerning nationalism, patriotism, or devotion to the state. The reason for this lack of interest probably lies in the fact that most of his previous writings or sermons containing strong statements on nationalism had been produced during a time of great emotional stress for Schleiermacher. In this sense of the word his nationalistic outbursts and interpretations had not been voluntary, but rather had resulted

[21] Schleiermacher to Henrietta Herz from Stolpe, April, 1804, Reimer (ed.), *Aus Schleiermachers Leben,* I, 394–395.

from pressures brought upon him by circumstances over which he had
had no control. When he moved to Halle the problems of the romanticists, the rationalists, the Pietists, and even the theologians faded into
the past and with them went the deep concentration he had devoted to
them. It was almost as though his nationalism was held in a state of
suspended animation for two years, awaiting a change in environment
before it could resume its growth. The tragic war which erupted in 1806
between Prussia and France thus became the most vital incident in his
life as a nationalist because it ended once and for all the peace and con-
tentment he had briefly experienced at Halle; Schleiermacher was pro-
jected upon a dynamic patriotic course which he followed for over a decade.

War between Prussia and France was not wholly unexpected in 1806,
even though Prussia had been only a casual spectator in the conflicts between France and the major European powers since 1795. In that year
Prussia had signed the Treaty of Basel and had thereby agreed to become
a neutral power. She carefully observed the rules of neutrality until
1805, when she belatedly joined a coalition against France involving
Russia, England, and Austria. Suspecting that the alliance was being arranged against him, Napoleon quickly moved to limit its effectiveness by
demanding a declaration of neutrality from Austria. When Austria refused to accept neutrality or to withdraw from the alliance Napoleon
moved his armies toward the Danube. In October, 1805, General Mack
von Leiberich surrendered 27,000 Austrian troops to the French at Ulm.
Prussia tardily joined the coalition against France, signing the Treaty of
Potsdam on November 3, 1805, but it was too late for her to render effective aid to Austria. Napoleon defeated the combined armies of Austria and Russia at the famous battle of Austerlitz on December 2, 1805,
and the coalition against France was for all practical purposes at an end.

Prussia's secret treaty with Austria and Russia placed her in an awkward position, for relations between France and Prussia had steadily deteriorated since the Treaty of Amiens in 1802, and by 1806 there seemed
little reason for the two countries to trust one another. When Napoleon
occupied Hanover and the ports of Cuxhaven and Ritzebüttel at the
mouth of the Elbe on June 3, 1803, Prussia had been helpless. Even when
the French kidnapped Sir George Rumbold, the British envoy at Ham-
burg, Friedrich Wilhelm could do little more than register a protest with
the French authorities. Because of breaches of faith like these Prussia
felt thoroughly justified in opening the negotiations with Austria and

Russia which resulted in the secret Treaty of Potsdam. The resounding defeat of the Russian and Austrian armies at Austerlitz should have discouraged Prussia concerning the possibility of further military action against Napoleon, for Prussia could easily see that she was no match for the armies of France. It seems reasonable to believe that Prussia would have accepted the Pressburg settlement and a position of continued subservience to France in 1806 if it had not been for the creation of the Confederation of the Rhine by Napoleon. When the French emperor fabricated this union of German states as an obvious thrust at Austria and Prussia, Friedrich Wilhelm saw no alternative but to mobilize the armies of Prussia and defend what little honor the country still retained.

When Prussia assembled her forces in August of 1806 she had Russia and Great Britain as allies; her military situation was far from hopeless. But before these allies could move to assist Prussia the French armies advanced into Prussian territory and Prussia was forced to bear the full impact of the French campaign. On October 14, 1806, when the French were victorious under Davout at Auerstädt and under Napoleon at Jena, Prussia simply wilted as a result of the defeats. Within a month all of Prussia's main fortifications were in French hands. Russia finally came to Prussia's aid in January, 1807, only to be defeated at Eylau on February 8, 1807, and again at Friedland on June 14, 1807. Having experienced enough carnage for the sake of Prussia, Alexander met with Napoleon to discuss a settlement of the conflict. The resulting negotiations produced the Treaty of Tilsit, which reduced Prussia to a weak state between the Elbe and Oder Rivers, severely limited her standing army, and permitted French occupation until an indemnity was paid. Prussia's humiliation over the haste with which her armies had surrendered in 1806 had been compounded by the fact that Russia and France did not even allow her to participate in the negotiation of the Tilsit agreements. War always brings drastic changes in the lives of the people of the nations involved, with the greatest changes usually being of a psychological nature. In the case of Friedrich Schleiermacher, this war and the resulting humiliation of Prussia in battle and at the peace table turned him into a fiery, determined, and unyielding patriot.

Like most Prussians, Schleiermacher had not concerned himself with the European wars between 1795 and 1805. These wars had seemed far away and of little concern to the average Prussian after Prussia signed the Treaty of Basel in 1795. When this Treaty was made public Schleiermacher preached a sermon in which he made reference to the Treaty as though it was an act to remove his country from the intricate involvements of European diplomacy.[22] This sermon contained absolutely none of the fervor that was noticeable after 1806. Schleiermacher also indicated in this sermon that he had been able to make no clear distinction between his loyalty to Prussia and his pride in his German culture. This inability to distinguish between the two types of loyalty was obvious when he defended the Treaty in 1795 because it would enable his "small fatherland" to go its way as a separate entity within the "large fatherland." In 1795 Schleiermacher was thus perfectly willing to let the rest of Germany go its own way so long as Prussia was at peace. However, by 1799, when he published his *Speeches on Religion,* this attitude of indifference had undergone a noticeable change. In this work he not only acknowledged that there was a common tie uniting Germans into a cultural bond, but he also proudly announced that the cultural heritage which dwelled in the breast of every German was superior to that of other national groups. The obvious transition in his thinking from the indifference of 1795 to the broad general national pride of 1799 became even more decidedly pronounced by 1805, for by that time he had reached the point where he was sure that Prussia and the rest of Germany had a common destiny as a German people. Still, he somehow could not separate the particular interests of Prussia from the national interests of a unified Germany.

Even before the beginning of the war with France in 1806 Schleiermacher realized that his own feelings about Germany were reaching a place where he would have to clarify his thinking concerning Prussia and Germany. As early as June, 1806, he caught a vision of the possibilities for Germany inherent in the anticipated conflict and he experienced a strange exhilaration from it. If France were to attack Prussia—and Schleiermacher had every reason to believe that this would be the case— the struggle would be a war for freedom for not only Prussia, but for all of Germany. As Friedrich told a close friend, there might be a day when everyone in Germany would be called upon to sacrifice everything he possessed. The price might seem high, but when a nation faced the loss of everything it had, any sacrifice would be justified. Having long advocated the freedom of the individual, he now said that everything was to be dedicated to the freedom of the nation because "the individual

---

[22] "Unregung zum Danke gegen Gott wegen der Wohltat des wiedergeschenkten Friedens," in Schleiermacher, *Sämmtliche Werke, Predigten,* VII, 340–353.

cannot go on existing, and can do nothing toward saving himself, if he should lose the German freedom and German feeling."[23] Schleiermacher was saying that Prussia could not exist as a separate state if the rest of Germany was to face destruction at the hands of a foreign country, although he was certainly not yet ready to acknowledge the dependence of Prussia upon the whole of Germany.

In anticipating a war with France, Schleiermacher saw the need for Prussians to demonstrate a high degree of patriotism toward their state. Shortly before the realities of war dawned upon the Prussian people he preached a sermon at Halle to the university students on the subject of their devotion to the state. According to him, the Jacobins of France had caused the very word "patriotism" to be discredited. They had created the impression that patriotism would inevitably lead the citizen to become obsessed with the welfare of his own country, creating a deep and lasting contempt for other nations and their citizens. That the French had perverted the meaning of patriotism was not proof that there was something wrong with being devoted to one's country, only that there was something wrong with the way the French utilized patriotism for impure purposes. Schleiermacher explained that patriotism was like human love. When love had been abused in human relationships, one did not blame the experience of love. Blame always fell instead upon those who had abused their freedom. If there were any faults connected with patriotism, these faults lay with an improper sense of direction in the patriot. Instead of causing contempt for other peoples, a properly directed sense of patriotism should make one have a greater respect for them. Schleiermacher confessed that he had tried to approach humanity from a cosmopolitan point of view when he had been deeply involved in studying Kant and Spinoza. He advised his listeners that he had learned from this experience with cosmopolitanism that one can never develop a true appreciation of mankind from such a broad approach. This appreciation would be established, he insisted, only by a realization of the worth of one's own people and culture. As far as Schleiermacher was concerned the man who failed to feel concern for his own land forfeited the right to criticize the ways and customs of any other people. He pointed out that since the Bible clearly revealed that the genuine spirit of Christ could never be in any person until that person had come to feel

---

[23] Schleiermacher to Charlotte von Kathen from Halle, June 20, 1806, Reimer (ed.), *Aus Schleiermachers Leben*, II, 63–64.

respect for his fellow man, at home and in foreign countries, one could not really experience Christianity without having a feeling of patriotism toward his country.[24]

It is difficult to tell if Schleiermacher meant that greater Prussian patriotism would increase the Prussian citizen's appreciation of the rest of Germany, or if he meant that greater patriotism by Prussians for Germany would increase the average German's respect for other countries. Whichever may have been the case, Schleiermacher was still thinking in terms of Prussian considerations first and German considerations second. He knew that the war, if it came, would not be between Frenchmen and Germans, but rather between Frenchmen and Prussians. Eventually the struggle would turn into a European war, but only after Prussia had taken the first shock of battle. Germany might be involved, but Prussian soldiers would be the ones called upon to give their lives before anyone else. Only eventually would the war involve the sentiments, religious culture, outward liberties, and worldly goods of the German people. Schleiermacher seemed to be thinking only of Prussia in this context; yet he referred to the impending war between Prussia and France as "the crisis in Germany" and proudly asserted that Germany was, after all, the very heart of Europe.[25]

Since he was looking upon German traditions as superior, and upon Prussia as somehow the perfect embodiment of this German spirit, one can easily see how profoundly Schleiermacher was shocked when, almost without a struggle, Prussia disintegrated before the French armies in October, 1806. Prussia's defeats on the battlefields of Jena and Auerstädt opened the way for the French armies to advance toward Halle, and on October 17 the forward elements of the French armies overran the Prussian positions outside the city and captured the main bridges over the Saale River. The events in Schleiermacher's life which followed the French attack upon Halle did what no amount of speculation had been able to do, for he quite suddenly had to rely upon the strength of nationalism in order to survive.

In the company of Henrik Steffens, a close friend and teaching associate from the University of Halle, Schleiermacher witnessed the battle for the main bridge leading into the city. They became so engrossed in

---

[24] "Wie sehr es die Würde des Menschen erhöht, wenn er mit ganzer Seele an der bürgerlichen Vereinigung hängt, der er angehört," in Schleiermacher, *Sämmtliche Werke, Predigten,* I, 223–231.

[25] Schleiermacher to Charlotte von Kathen from Halle, June 20, 1806, Reimer (ed.), *Aus Schleiermachers Leben,* II, 64.

the fighting that they stayed too long and were consequently caught between the Prussian and French armies as the Prussians retreated. Making their way to Schleiermacher's quarters, they found that they were
no more safe than they had been, for the "imprudence of the people who
live beneath enabled a number of hussars to break into the house and
make their way upstairs to our rooms." Steffens and Schleiermacher had
been joined by Joachim Gass from the University of Halle and the
French soldiers forced all three of them to give up their watches and
their money. Schleiermacher's only satisfaction in the affair was that he
was so poor at the time that the soldiers got only a few thalers from him,
but the French compensated for this by taking all but two of his shirts.[26]

The personal danger he had experienced in the streets and the fear he
had felt when the soldiers entered his room and demanded his money
were only an introduction to what was to come. The night after the
battle and the next few days were just one long, unbroken period of
agony and frustration. Schleiermacher was forced to billet a number of
soldiers in his quarters, which were already crowded with the presence
of his landlord and several orphans under the guardianship of two elderly
women. All articles of value had been taken from these people and
Schleiermacher feared that irresponsible actions such as this pillaging,
if reproduced all over Halle, might drive the citizens to attempt some
desperate act of revenge. Knowing that such an uprising by the citizenry
could only lead to a blockade, he spent some of the most anxious days of
his life waiting for the worst to happen. The discomforts of the cramped
quarters was increased when Schleiermacher had to quarter the secretary of the French military staff and two other employees, who passed
their leisure by frightening the lodgers with threats that they were going
to put Halle to the torch after they had plundered the town.[27] Having
to sit helplessly and endure this type of treatment at the hands of the
French did more than just make Friedrich angry. It built in him a loath-
ing for the French, and at the same time it implanted in him a growing
disgust for the weakness of Prussia. He knew that the unwillingness of
the Prussians to defend their land was as much a cause for the humiliating days and nights with the French as was the strength of the Napoleonic armies.

The disgust and disillusionment of defeat turned to dismay when
Friedrich learned that the French had ordered the dispersion of the stu-

[26] Schleiermacher to Georg Reimer from Halle, November 4, 1806, *ibid.*, II,
71.
[27] See *ibid.*

dents from the University of Halle. On October 18, 1806, a deputation composed of Maass, Schmalz, Eberhard, Knapp, and Froriep pleaded with Marshal Bernadotte to keep the University open. At that time only Marshals Lannes, Augereau, and Bernadotte had arrived in Halle, for Napoleon did not enter the city until October 19. Bernadotte was apparently sympathetic to the pleas of the delegation, but he was powerless as far as making any long-term commitment was concerned.[28] The uncertainty concerning the future of the University of Halle drove Schleiermacher to the depths of despair, for he knew that his career there was at an end. He stated so in a letter to a friend in Berlin, "Even if peace comes soon, Halle will probably not remain Prussian. If it should be given to Saxony, then probably the university will be dissolved, or at any rate it will end my stay here, for the Saxons are very strict Lutherans."[29] If Halle went to the French, he would certainly have to leave, for he would never be able to live in French territory "as long as there is a Prussian hole somewhere to which I can retreat."[30]

No matter how he looked at his situation in Halle, Friedrich saw that his teaching career was about to come to an end because of the French, who had turned his promising work at Halle into a "ruined activity, which will probably never again be restored." If he would be turned into a wandering vagabond as he predicted, where would he go? His uncertainty about Halle was overshadowed by the total absence of any information about the progress of the war. He even looked upon the blackout of the news as another French trick to break the spirit of Halle's citizens. Of this lack of news he wrote to a friend, "Our utter ignorance of the state of affairs since the fall of Potsdam and Berlin is terrifying, and surely is calculated to dampen our spirit and paralyze our last energies."[31]

This was one of the darkest hours for Schleiermacher. Like many Germans he saw the foundations of his life swept away. His country had failed miserably in a test of its manhood; his career as a teacher was ruined before it was little more than started; his personal pride had been crushed by crude treatment of his friends and associates—yet through it all he had been helpless. In his despair he turned back to the moments when he had been forced to end his relationship with Eleanor Grünow.

[28] Dilthey, *Leben Schleiermachers,* pp. 814–816.
[29] Schleiermacher to Georg Reimer from Halle, November 4, 1806, Reimer (ed.), *Aus Schleiermachers Leben,* II, 71–72.
[30] *Ibid.,* II, 71–72.
[31] Schleiermacher to Henrietta Herz from Halle, November 4, 1806, *ibid.,* II, 73.

Just as she had been unwilling to make a sacrifice for his sake and seek a divorce from her husband, perhaps Prussia might prove to be untrue in its hour of crisis. He knew that there was a distinct possibility that even Prussia, his own country, might prove to be so weak that it would no longer merit his patriotism. He was dangerously close to the point where a man no longer has faith in any human institution, but even in his darkest hour he never lost faith in Friedrich Wilhelm III and the queen. His greatest desire in late 1806 was that he might be able to see the King in order to speak a word of encouragement to him.

The winter of 1806 was not just a winter of mental anguish for the young Halle preacher. It was also a time of physical privation. After the salaries of the professors at the University of Halle were cut off in December, 1806, even the basic necessities of life became scarce in his house. Such basic essentials as firewood became difficult to acquire and the specter of famine was a reality for many in Halle that winter. Friedrich had been forced to give all his cash to the French but managed to secure a small amount from the travel box of Gass, who had left Halle and made his way to Stettin through the French lines. When this small amount of money was gone Schleiermacher resorted to the barter system used by the other residents of Halle.[33]

In the midst of all of this suffering and difficulty he found himself asking the same question that others were asking of him as a preacher: Why does God allow His children to suffer? When the students of the University came seeking an answer to the suffering and heartbreak for Prussia which was a result of the war, Schleiermacher found, as had ministers through the ages, that there were no simple answers to give them. He knew that the students were not asking questions concerning Prussia's plight as a matter of speculation. These queries were compassionate pleas from the depths of the soul of a whole people searching, seeking to regain solid ground in the midst of confusion. With a compassion equal to that of his students he sought the same answers as they did. That is why one must look at his sermons to see how Schleiermacher came to recognize the true value of German nationalism, because, as he tried to explain to his listeners at the chapel of the University of Halle why the ravages of war came to Prussia, he realized for the first time that only a unified Germany could have prevented the defeat.

[32] Schleiermacher to Henrietta Herz from Halle, November 14, 1806, *ibid.*, II, 74–75; Schleiermacher to Georg Reimer from Halle [no date], *ibid.*, II, 72; Dilthey, *Leben Schleiermachers,* p. 827.
[33] Dilthey, *Leben Schleiermachers*, pp. 821–827.

By way of introduction to the sermons in which Schleiermacher revealed a newly discovered awareness of Prussia's role in a German nation, one must look at a sermon which he had preached shortly before
the struggle began in 1806. In picturing for his congregation the foundations that make a nation strong, he said at that time that the family, the
church, and the nation were only different levels of individualism. The
highest individuality was that which is achieved when the individual
loses his own particular identity in the group. The highest type of group
according to Schleiermacher was the nation. Accordingly, work within
the group which formed the nation became important regardless of how
lowly a form it might take. The customs and the time-honored institutions of the whole nation were thus only the total results of all the lives
of the people in the nation. Although these manifestations of individuality often bore little resemblance to the national character, nevertheless
each act by an individual was a part of the process of building the nation.[34]

Evidently he had never tried to apply this idea of submergence within
the group to the Prussian state, for if he had he would have seen that just
as the individual actually gains from losing his individualism in the
group, and the group gains by losing its identity in the nation, so then
the particular German states like Prussia also would gain by losing their
particular identity in a German nation. In fact, he never seemed to question the nature of the relationship between the various German states
until the defeats of 1806 forced him to do so. When he tried to answer
the searching inquiries of his students, and at the same time attempted
to find solace for his own mind, he decided that the tragedies of 1806 had
come to Prussia because something was wrong with the structure of the
Prussian state. Under the burden of personal privation and disillusionment Schleiermacher passed a crisis in his development as a nationalist
when he began to question the existence of Prussia as his fatherland.

Schleiermacher first indicated his belief that the war was an act of
God to awaken the people of Prussia to their destiny in Germany in two
sermons which he preached in Halle on November 16, 1806, and November 23, 1806.[35] In these sermons he reasoned that by His very nature,
God is love. Thus every act of God, even that which might resemble

---

[34] "Wie sehr es die Würde des Menschen erhöht, wenn er mit ganzer Seele an
der bürgerlichen Vereinigung hängt, der er angehört," in Schleiermacher,
Sämmtliche Werke, Predigten, I, 225–231.

[35] "Das überall Frieden ist im Reiche Gottes" and Über die Benutzung öffent-
licher Unglücksfalle" in Schleiermacher, Sämmtliche Werke, Predigten, I, 239–
265.

punishment, is a revelation of His love. In the same way that God loved the individual man, He also loved the composite man, the nation. Consequently, God must allow certain events to occur in dealing with states which may seem to be misfortunes to the people, but which are actually intended to move the state toward a higher goal. Schleiermacher confessed that he did not know precisely what lay in store for Prussia, but he was relatively sure that either a change in the internal structure of the Prussian state or an alteration of the relationship between Prussia and other German states would be in order before peace would ever be granted to the people of North Germany.

Schleiermacher pursued this line of thought even further in a letter to a friend about the same time that he preached these sermons. He indicated in the letter that he was starting to realize that if Prussia were destroyed, then all Protestant German states would be in danger because Prussia was a cornerstone for German Protestantism. Not only would all of Protestant Germany suffer from the loss of Prussian freedom of religion, but all of Protestant Germany would eventually have to stand together to drive the French out. He was on the verge of calling for a national German crusade when he said, "The rod of wrath must descend upon the hand of *every German,* for it is only as a result of a situation like this that a proud and glorious future will blossom."[36] Schleiermacher was obviously thinking in terms of the need for the rest of Germany to come to the aid of Prussia, but he seems to have been thinking only in terms of Protestant Germany, for little that he said could be applied to Catholic areas of South Germany or West Germany. Nevertheless, he was projecting the tragedy of 1806 against a picture of a national movement by German people. Still unclear in Schleiermacher's thinking was the way that Prussia would fit into this "national movement." He had seemingly ignored the ramifications of the "national uprising" he was proposing on behalf of Prussia. Especially unclear in late 1806 was the question of whether Germany should help Prussia restore her former position, or whether Prussia and the German states should strive for a unified German state. In either case, he was thinking in terms of Prussia as the leader in any such "German" movement.

Schleiermacher's humiliation over Prussia's defeat thus deepened his determination to help resist the deterioration which he saw taking place all around him. One factor which helped him steady his will to resist what he saw happening in Prussian society under the impact of the

[36] Schleiermacher to Henrietta Herz from Halle, November 21, 1806, Reimer (ed.), *Aus Schleiermachers Leben,* II, 76, italics added.

French invasion and the occupation was the attitude of the students at
Halle. In the presence of Napoleon the Halle students shouted praises
for the King of Prussia and hissed the Emperor. The French soldiers in
turn tried to drown out the shouts of the students by crying "Vive
L'Empereur.[37] The result was a vocal tug of war which was handily won
by the students. Of course such a demonstration by the Halle students
meant the end of any hope for restoration of the university to its former
status, but for the University preacher it was another in a long series of
events moving him toward an open avowal of German nationalism. He
decided that the defiant spirit of the students was symbolic of what all of
Prussia must experience before the French would ever be expelled from
Prussian soil. Believing that the spirit of the Halle students was the basis
for hope for a German movement against France, he left for Berlin,
where he felt that he could be useful in arousing a disillusioned, defeated
Prussia to take advantage of the dedication of her youth. He went to the
Prussian capital with the assurance that the testing time for Prussia and
all of Germany had arrived. He knew that constitutional changes might
be necessary before Prussia could lead Germany to make a united effort
against Napoleon, and that the monarchy was possibly an outdated institution which would have to be altered. Regardless of what had to be
sacrificed, Germany must prove that from the destruction of her peaceful state she could extract a kernel worth saving. He expressed these
views beautifully when, in connection with his move to Berlin and his
hopes for Prussian leadership in Germany, he said, "I feel sure that Germany, the kernel of Europe, will arise once more in a new and beautiful
state, but when this will happen, and whether the country will not first
have to experience even greater difficulties . . . God alone knows."[38]

The hopeful minister making his way to Berlin in 1807 was thus a man
far different from the young author who had inadvertently touched upon
some nationalistic topics in a book on religion in 1800. Because of the
assurance and confidence he had gained from the publication of *Speeches
on Religion* and *Soliloquies* and because of the intellectual stimulation
of his departure from the romantic circle, he had begun to search out
the significance of the unusual pride he possessed concerning his German
heritage. Then an unusual set of events placed him in a position to experience the full impact of the defeat of Prussia at the hands of France
in 1806. Seeing that Prussia could not deal with France without the aid

[37] Dilthey, *Leben Schleiermachers*, p. 818.
[38] Schleiermacher to Ehrenfried von Willich, December 1, 1806, Reimer (ed.),
Aus Schleiermachers Leben, II, 80.

of other German states and recognizing that Prussia's plight was a blow to all of Germany, he was determined to arouse all of Germany to come to the aid of Prussia, and under Prussia's leadership drive France from the soil of Germany. He had not been able to differentiate by 1807 between Prussian particularism and German nationalism, but he was only a step away from discovering that the various German states would never be willing to sacrifice their young men for the sake of Prussian particularism. Veit Valentin described this situation well in his book, *The German People,*[39] when he said that the problem for men like Schleiermacher was:

. . . how to make the full, deep mature personal culture of German classicism fruitful in forming German national feeling. The Prussian state needed German intellect; it demanded Prussian fighters to rebuild Prussia as a great power, but they could be won only by arousing self-awareness of the homogeneousness of the German people—and they by putting it to work. . . . Prussia had a German vocation; she could not advance without German idealism, and yet the most powerful social groups in Prussia set their old-style Prussianism above the collective fatherland; they developed a Prussian patriotism at the expense of German patriotism.[40]

Though Schleiermacher would come to see that Prussian particularism would not answer the needs of Prussia, let alone lead to the unification of the German people, his attitude in 1807 was basically that described by Valentin. This was the stage to which his German nationalism had developed when he moved to Berlin in 1807.

[39] Veit Valentin, *The German People,* p. 340.
[40] *Ibid.*

The story of Friedrich Schleiermacher's life from 1807 until 1811 is one of frustration and dismay as he tried to bring about the regeneration of patriotic spirit in Prussia. During this period he tried with as much determination as any man could have possessed to encourage the political leaders of his country to assert themselves and rally the German spirit of the people. He could not perceive that he was seeking the impossible. Only after five years of failure was he finally able to see through the false assumptions he had made about the relationship of Prussia to the rest of Germany. Without a doubt the last step in his evolutionary process toward nationalism, that of discarding Prussian patriotism for German nationalism, was the most difficult to achieve, but once he came to recognize German nationalism as the first allegiance in his life he took on an entirely new outlook.

This period of his life was marked by failure. Almost everything that Schleiermacher attempted for the good of Prussia failed. However, his efforts were of great significance for the development of his nationalism because each failure taught him the limitations of particularism. Only after being stymied at every turn in his efforts to arouse a nationalistic zeal in Prussia did he finally concede the point that only a genuine spirit of national devotion to a unified Germany could achieve the goals he had envisioned for Prussia.

Schleiermacher's first opportunity to help rebuild Prussia came in November, 1807, when he was notified by the Prussian government that as soon as a new university could be established to replace Halle he would be asked to join its faculty. The best that the government could offer him until that time was a stipend equal to half of what he had received at Halle. Faced with what might develop into a long period of unemployment, he spent most of 1808 in search of means to supplement his meager income.[1] But even while he was lecturing on the classics, preaching at various Berlin churches, and writing, he was actively seeking some way to bolster Prussian resistance to the French occupation. Since he was already well known in Berlin as a result of his books and his years spent in preaching there, and since he let his desires to work for Prussia be known, he was soon asked to join one of the secret societies which had been recently organized in Prussia for the purpose of driving the French out of the country. A man by the name of Bearsch, representing the Moral and Scientific Union, or as it was better known, the Tugendbund, approached him about joining the society, presenting him with a copy of the constitution so that Friedrich might study the nature and purposes of the organization. Even though the society had been organized in Königsberg by highly reputable Prussians like Gneisenau, Grolmann, and Krug, Schleiermacher refused to join it because doing so would compromise his convictions about the undesirability of belonging to secret organizations. He also felt that the society would be useless in the hands of sincere men, and as dangerous as the Jacobin Club if it ever fell under the control of men with unscrupulous political motives.[2]

The Tugendbund was only one of the many ultranationalistic organizations which came into existence in Germany in 1807 and 1808 after Prussia had been forced to accept the extremely harsh terms of the Tilsit agreement between France and Russia. Most of these societies were financed with English funds, were rather informal in their structure, and were dedicated to the task of ridding Prussia of the French, with the aid of Austria, the German states, and England.[3]

Although Schleiermacher refused to join the Tugendbund, he soon became active in another secret organization in Berlin known as the Charlottenburger Verein, which was a segment of a larger secret organization in Berlin known as the Party of Patriots [Patriotenpartei]. This larger society, of which Scharnhorst, Gneisenau, and Stein were members, was led by a number of military and political officials who were determined to resist Napoleon and some day drive him and his armies

[1] "Schleiermachers politische Gesinnung und Wirksamkeit," in Wilhelm Dilthey, *Wilhelm Diltheys Gesammelte Schriften*, XII, 16: "An den Herrn Geheimenrath Schmalz," in Friedrich Schleiermacher, *Sämmtliche Werke, Zur Philosophie*, IX, 645–664.

[2] John R. Seeley, *The Life and Times of Stein*, II, 79–89; "An der Herrn Geheimenrath Schmalz," in Schleiermacher, *Sämmtliche Werke, Zur Philosophie*, IX, 655–665.

[3] "Schleiermachers politische Gesinnung und Wirksamkeit," in Dilthey, *Gesammelte Schriften*, XII, 25.

out of Prussia. Preparing for a military campaign by training a forbidden army under the noses of the French officials and spies in Prussia was a most difficult and dangerous task to undertake. Even the most elemental diplomacy necessary to gain support from England and Austria was hazardous, for anyone caught in the act of creating opposition to Napoleon could expect swift punishment.

Not only must foreign aid be enlisted for an armed uprising against France, but the northern German states had to be sounded out about their military dispositions in case Prussia was to renew her struggle against France. Because of the complexity of organizing effective resistance against Napoleon and because of the need for secrecy, the Party of Patriots organized committees to keep in contact with one another and to establish a means of communication between cities. In addition to being clearing houses for information, they also served as planning centers for drawing up various tactical operations to be used against the French if war was to start.[4]

The small society to which Schleiermacher belonged, the Charlottenburger Verein, consisted primarily of military figures who were preparing for the eventuality of an insurrection and were grooming themselves for places of leadership. Dealing as they did with the planning of military operations, they risked their lives in just coming together. Consequently there were no membership records and Friedrich himself was not sure about the names of the people in the society or of how many were active in its work.[5]

A great many Prussians shared Schleiermacher's optimism about the ease with which they could expel France from their country, basing this optimism upon the seeming weakness of Napoleon's military position in Europe in 1808. The French had appeared to be invulnerable at Tilsit in July, 1807, but at that very time they were experiencing grave difficulties in Spain. The festering sore of rebellion in Spain became so serious in 1808 that it was a source of extreme embarrassment for Napoleon and at the same time a source of tremendous encouragement for occupied areas like Prussia. The Spanish revolt proved that it was virtually impossible for a country like France to control a mass of people infused with a spirit of nationalism.

Stein and other Prussian leaders, firmly convinced that Prussia could

[4] *Ibid.*, XII, 23–25.
[5] Ernst Müsebeck, *Ernst Moritz Arndt: Ein Lebensbild*, 236–269; Seeley, *The Life and Times of Stein*, II, 89–90; "An den Herrn Geheimenrath Schmalz," in Schleiermacher, *Sämmtliche Werke, Zur Philosophie*, IX, 645–666.

duplicate the achievements of the Spanish, decided to take advantage of Napoleon's preoccupation with Spain by forming an alliance with Austria. Napoleon was, of course, not blind to what was taking place in Prussia, and he moved to apply pressure directly upon Friedrich Wilhelm III by demanding that Prussia limit the size of its army and pay France a huge indemnity. Faced with Napoleon's determination to keep a careful watch over Prussia in spite of the difficulties he was experiencing in Spain, the Prussian government had two clear-cut alternatives. It could accept Napoleon's terms with the humiliation that would accompany them, or it could continue to work toward a military alliance with Austria.

Being unsure of Prussia's ability to sustain a revolutionary movement against France, and being equally unsure of the state of Austria's military preparations, Friedrich Wilhelm decided to confer with Alexander of Russia before he reached a decision for or against an Austrian alliance. If there was any possibility that Russia might renew hostilities against France, Friedrich Wilhelm III would consider this as reason enough to conclude an alliance with Austria. Because of the importance of learning quickly the attitude of Russia, Friedrich Wilhelm could not rely upon normal channels of diplomacy, but at the same time he could not risk a personal trip to Russia for fear that such a trip would force the hand of Napoleon. Fortunately for Prussia, Alexander would spend a week at Königsberg on his way to Erfurt to have a conference with Napoleon, which meant that it would be possible to carry on negotiations with the Czar without arousing the suspicion of Napoleon. Friedrich Wilhelm III felt that he would be able to determine from the results of the discussion whether to continue his efforts toward making an alliance with Austria or whether he should try to reach some satisfactory compromise with the French.

As soon as the Party of Patriots learned that Alexander was to be in Königsberg they could visualize tremendous results from the negotiations. Since any agreement reached at Königsberg would bear directly upon the activities of the patriotic committees in Berlin, the Party of Patriots decided to send a messenger to represent them during the talks. Realizing the need for selecting the least likely person for the responsibility of serving as a diplomatic courier in order to fool the French spies, and seeing at the same time that this courier must be a man who was dedicated to the cause of reviving the prestige of Prussia, the Party of Patriots selected Friedrich Schleiermacher as their envoy to Königsberg.

Schleiermacher placed a great deal of hope in the mission on which he was being sent, for he was laboring under the belief that all Prussia needed was the help of a foreign power such as Russia in order to begin a war with the French. Once a power like Russia came to Prussia's aid, the other German states would naturally rush to the aid of Friedrich Wilhelm III, and France would be driven from Germany. The fact that he was anticipating the impossible did not seem to enter his mind as the representative of the Party of Patriots made his way eastward to Königsberg; nor did he seem concerned with the possibility that the mission might be a failure. He was operating under what Carlton J. H. Hayes referred to as "nationalistic faith,"[6] in that he believed if Germany started moving in the right direction, all the problems of unification would solve themselves. He revealed this tendency to oversimplify the prerequisite ingredients for a national awakening in Germany when he wrote to Henrietta von Willich shortly after arriving at his destination in East Prussia, that if he had doubted the purpose for which he had come to Königsberg he would have been unworthy of the love she had for him, because he would have been a traitor to Prussia and to all of Germany. He was proud that in assuming the dangerous task of acting as a courier he was leading Germany one step closer to freedom and unity.[7]

Taking into account the misguided but nevertheless sincere faith that he had placed in the negotiations at Königsberg, one can easily visualize the profound effect the failure of the talks would have upon him. Contrary to all the predictions that the theologian-turned-diplomat made concerning the ease with which Alexander could be won over to Prussia's side,[8] during the September talks the Czar refused to renounce his alliance with Napoleon. Alexander's action in turn led Friedrich Wilhelm to decide against any further negotiations for a treaty with Austria. About all that Prussia was able to salvage from the Königsberg conversations was a promise from Alexander to speak on Prussia's behalf at the Erfurt meeting with Napoleon. Schleiermacher, having expected so much from the meeting of the sovereigns and seeing so little in the way of results, returned to Berlin in a state of deep gloom. His first effort to arouse the fighting spirit of Prussia had been a failure. Instead of a revolution and a restoration of Prussian freedom, there was only a mis-

---

[6] Carlton J. H. Hayes, *Essays on Nationalism*, pp. 105–106.

[7] Schleiermacher to Henrietta von Willich from Königsberg, September 11, 1808, Georg Reimer (ed.), *Aus Schleiermachers Leben in Briefen*, II, 132.

[8] Schleiermacher to Georg Reimer from Königsberg, September 6, 1808, Heinrich Meisner (ed.), *Schleiermacher als Mensch: Sein Werden und Wirken, Familien-und Freundesbriefe*, II, 110–112.

erable agreement with Alexander—the same man who had helped put Prussia in her subservient position.[9]

The repercussions of the failure of the Königsberg mission upon Schleiermacher's nationalistic outlook were tremendous, even though he did not readily see the full implications of what he had learned from the experience. First of all, he could see that Prussia was incapable of initiating any action against France. The Prussians had to go begging at the conference table and had to be satisfied with the miserable crumbs that might come their way. With the weakness of the Prussian military forces there was evidently no way in the immediate future for the country to build up the strength to defy Napoleon alone. Secondly, it was obvious that neither Europe in general, nor the German states in particular, were the least bit concerned with the future of Prussia. It would take three years for Schleiermacher to admit the obvious fact that Prussia could not command the respect of the major powers of Europe. Until that time he would continue to believe that he could cling to his hopes of a unified Germany led by a strong Prussian state. Thirdly, even Schleiermacher should have been able to see at Königsberg that no amount of courage and determination by Prussians like himself could result in an awakening of German nationalism, for even he was thinking only in terms of Prussian particularism. Although he did not immediately admit the inadequacies of his narrow Prussian approach to German nationalism, the failures of the Königsberg mission created serious doubts in his mind concerning Prussia's leadership, and these doubts would bear fruit later.

The first evidence that his doubts concerning Prussia's future were growing appeared in a letter which Schleiermacher wrote to Henrietta von Willich, with whom he had become engaged and whom he would marry in 1809. He told his fiancée that his life of service to the Church, science, or the state must never be placed above his relationship to her. Only a few months earlier he had told her that service to Prussia must be placed above all his responsibilities. Now he was saying in essence that since his services did not seem to make much difference as far as Prussia was concerned he would consider his family responsibilities above his other duties.[10] Such a pessimistic note did not mean that he had lost all hope for a better day for Prussia, but it certainly revealed a lack of confidence in any immediate changes in Prussia or Germany.

---

[9] "Schleiermachers politische Gesinnung und Wirksamkeit," in Dilthey, *Gesammelte Schriften*, XII, 26–32; Seeley, *The Life and Times of Stein*, II, 91–92.

[10] Schleiermacher to Henrietta von Willich from Berlin, October 22, 1808, Reimer (ed.), *Aus Schleiermachers Leben*, II, 152–153.

A month after Schleiermacher returned from his Königsberg trip an incident occurred which added to his conviction that it was useless for him to risk his life if nothing more could come from his efforts than the results he had seen in East Prussia. A French officer visited him at his home in Berlin and told him that Marshal Davout wished to speak with him. Two men, evidently summoned for the same purpose as Schleiermacher had been, were already in the carriage which was waiting for him. The officer took the three men to the headquarters of the French occupational forces. There Davout delivered to them a stern lecture, during the course of which he accused them of provoking disorders and acting as troublemakers. Following the lecture Friedrich was allowed to return home without any formal charges being made against him. Having good reason to believe that the French had some knowledge of his secret activities with the Party of Patriots, he was, however, convinced that his usefulness to Prussia as a secret agent was at an end.[11]

The disillusionment which he experienced because the war against France did not materialize did not prevent his participation in activities other than personal diplomatic missions. When he saw that Prussia could not hope for help from any outside force such as Russia, he turned his attention to other means of building a sense of patriotism in Prussia. He still believed that Prussia could, and should, lead the rest of Germany in a war against France. Since the Königsberg mission had failed to produce an answer to Prussia's dilemma, he would simply have to search for another way of helping bring about a war against France. It was only after he had made every effort to arouse and stimulate German nationalism by appealing to Prussian patriotism that he realized he was dealing with the impossible. Only the total disillusionment resulting from having tried every conceivable means of arousing Prussian patriotism and from having failed in every effort could cause him to turn ultimately to the belief in German nationalism with no reservations, no particularist qualifications, and no idealistic predictions.

The first of these varied attempts at arousing patriotic activity following the Königsberg mission was a lecture series on patriotic topics.[12] The fact that practically nothing remains extant concerning these lectures except brief references in letters is understandable in the light of Schleiermacher's habit of never writing his sermons and lectures so that

[11] Schleiermacher to Henrietta von Willich from Berlin [October], 1808, *ibid.,* II, 175–176.
[12] Schleiermacher to Henrietta von Willich from Berlin, October 22, 1808, *ibid.,* II, 152–153.

they could be preserved. At any rate, this lecture series could have lasted only for a short time, for he was appointed to the pulpit of Trinity Church [Dreifaltigkeitskirche] in Berlin in 1809. His new responsibility gave him the economic security for which he had constantly sought, as well as a forum for extolling the virtues of patriotism. In the pulpit he had the opportunity from week to week to explain to his congregation the gravity of Prussia's plight and the country's need of dedicated men and women. The freedom of the Holy Desk gave him the chance to show his congregation, composed of some of the very finest and most influential people in Berlin, that they had an obligation to God and their fellow citizens which could never be fulfilled until Prussia was free from France. However, instead of motivating the people of his congregation to respond to the challenge of Prussian patriotism, he felt himself being infected by their lack of concern for Prussia and by the obvious indifference of the very people he was trying to transform. The seeming inability on Friedrich's part to find satisfaction in any type of service designed to foster patriotism helps explain why he finally turned to political service in the Prussian government as a sort of last-ditch effort to keep his own beliefs about patriotism alive. This is not to say that he was not interested in the political fortunes of Prussia before 1809, for he had been rather intimately associated with Baron von Stein's program of reforms since his arrival in Berlin from Halle, but it was not until late 1808 and early 1809 that he became personally involved in the government's reform program.

From the time when Friedrich Wilhelm had called Stein to take charge of the prostrate Prussian government after the disastrous Tilsit agreements in 1807 Schleiermacher had been in basic sympathy with the Baron's reform program. His admiration for Stein's reforms and the similarity between the views of the two men help explain why Schleiermacher was so pleased when he was called upon to assist the Baron in reforming the educational system in Prussia. But in order to understand why Stein was interested in having Schleiermacher participate in his efforts to reconstruct Prussia's educational processes, one must look closely at Schleiermacher's views on education. The Trinity Church pastor had already demonstrated in his books and his service at Halle that he was deeply interested in the need for an educational program which would create a sense of patriotic devotion on the part of the student. Of course, he had not been the first man in his time to see the value of a state-controlled school system for the growth of patriotism in the state; nor was he the first to point out the significant role which a study of the native language plays in building up a sense of national devotion. Nationalists like Herder had been quick to acknowledge the primary importance of language as a vehicle for transmitting the culture of a national group from one generation to another. Hayes neatly summed up the attitude of the nationalist with regard to language when he said that "a nationality receives its impress, its character, its individuality, not, unless very incidentally, from physical geography or biological race, but rather from cultural and historical forces. First and foremost among these I would put language."[13] A determined effort by the state to purify and use the language as a nationalistic tool had been advocated by other nationalists besides Schleiermacher, but he was one of the first to express the notion that educational reforms would be necessary before Prussia could become a nation of patriots. Long before the crisis of 1806 he had proposed sweeping reforms of the entire educational system. Even at the early date he had been painfully aware that the deficiencies of the Prussian educational system, as it was operated under ecclesiastical control, simply could not stand the strain of a national disaster.

Schleiermacher had started his efforts to improve the quality of the Prussian system when he demanded in his *Speeches on Religion* that the state assume control of a major portion of the educational activities then being supervised by the Church. He even had gone so far as to reject state help to Church schools where the Church-related subjects did not cover the needs of the pupils. As has already been noted in the second chapter, Schleiermacher opposed close Church-state relations in education because of the damaging effect the resulting state supervision had upon the Church. He had been equally firm in his opposition to the existing system in Prussia because he felt that it produced a haphazard process of education. With academic studies and applied sciences falling outside the interests of religious institutions, making these institutions teach specialized fields was to force upon them a task for which they were not equipped. He felt that the only hope for the religious institutions would be for them to refuse to teach fields for which they were not prepared and equipped, thus forcing the state to create institutions better suited for secular academic pursuits than were the Church-related schools. The Church institutions would then be left alone to care for theological education, and the state would omit from its course of study only those areas covered in the Church schools. The creation of state schools alongside the older ecclesiastical schools would not mean that

---

[13] Carlton J. H. Hayes, *Nationalism: A Religion,* p. 3.

there would be a decrease in the power or authority of the Church. Rather, as Schleiermacher saw it, this move would strengthen the Church because religious institutions would be free from the controls which had followed in the wake of responsibilities to the state.[14]

While the Church would gain a great deal from the creation of state institutions of learning, the state would gain far more. For a number of years the Prussian government had encouraged the Church institutions to expand and to intensify their work of public instruction. The Church, in turn, had been willing to render this service to the state, but both the Church and the state had become aware of the fact that there were certain liabilities for the state in letting the Church carry on the work of educating Prussia's youth. For instance, the ecclesiastical teachers continually experienced difficulties in reconciling Germany's history of war with the doctrine of love. When such conflicts arose the interests of the Church were given preference over national interests, the result being that the youth had not been given the background necessary to make them love their country. As long as education remained the prerogative of the Church this deplorable condition would continue.[15]

For some unexplainable reason Schleiermacher's ideas on the need for reforms in the Prussian educational system did not attract a great deal of attention before 1806. Perhaps the theological significance of his *Speeches on Religion* simply caused the educational theories in the book to become less important than they might have been if the book had been aimed primarily at reforms in education. Schleiermacher himself had very little to say concerning education between 1800 and 1806, generally making only a passing reference to it in connection with some other topic in his writings. Once, in 1802, he became so disgusted with prevailing methods of teaching that he started to write a textbook on education, but he evidently lost interest in the project and nothing resulted from it.[16]

Schleiermacher's first serious attempt after 1800 to relate Prussia's need for patriotic stimulation to the educational system of the state was in his review of a book by Friedrich Zöllner in 1805. In his *Ideas on National Education* Zöllner advanced the theory that the German language should be taught throughout Germany on a mandatory basis. He had a dual purpose in making such a demand. In the first place, German

[14]*Über die Religion* in Schleiermacher, *Sämmtliche Werke, Zur Theologie,* I, 374–375.
[15] *Ibid.,* I, 199–200.
[16] Schleiermacher to Eleanor Grünow from Stolpe, August 12, 1802, Reimer (ed.), *Aus Schleiermachers Leben,* I, 314–315.

would take the place of any other language being used in German states, such as Polish and Lithuanian in the eastern districts of Prussia. Secondly, on an even broader scale, he hoped that the use of the German language would help develop a national spirit among the German people.[17] Friedrich said in his review of Zöllner's book that the author was basically correct. Germany would never become conscious of a common destiny until it was conscious of common cultural ties. However, though Schleiermacher agreed with Zöllner on the need for language studies, he disagreed with him concerning the basic reason for studying the German language. Schleiermacher maintained that language studies in themselves would not satisfy the national needs of Germany. The state must not teach the German language; it must *use* the language. Language studies were not for him an end, but a means to an end. He called attention to the fact that Zöllner would actually defeat his own purpose if a national educational system was established for all of Germany, because the diversity of German traditions would make it impossible to devise a system of language studies which would satisfactorily transmit German traditions. The governments of the separate German states would have to consider each group of children separately because each area had its own cultural heritage which would have to be studied and utilized.[18]

These brief samples of Schleiermacher's thoughts on education reveal the same inability to apply nationalistic principles to the whole of Germany as had troubled him in the field of political activity. He was seemingly unable to think in terms of anything larger than Prussia without dealing in vague generalities. Yet his grasp of the basic needs for educational reforms in Prussia made so great an impression upon Stein that when the reformer decided to reorganize the entire school system of Prussia one of the first men he appointed to a special group to study the reorganization was Schleiermacher. Friedrich was joined on the committee by a number of talented and imaginative men, among them Fichte, Nicolovius, Wilhelm von Humboldt, and Karl August von Hardenberg, who like Schleiermacher had attracted attention because of their concern over the need for educational reforms in Prussia.

The key figure in Stein's educational reforms was Humboldt, a prophet of doom for systems like benevolent despotism and enlightened absolutism before the French Revolution began. He had based his beliefs on the idea that neither governments nor people prosper on re-

[17] Salo W. Baron, *Modern Nationalism and Religion*, p. 133.
[18] Koppel Pinson, *Pietism as a Factor in the Rise of German Nationalism*, p. 146.

forms based on rational processes. He wanted only acts which produced immediate results. When he saw France undergo the horrors of the Reign of Terror because of attempts to create a perfect society, he became more convinced than ever that men could not reason themselves into perfection. In addition to generally disliking republican principles, Humboldt, through his close association with Goethe and Schiller, acquired an aversion for the applied principles of rationalism and republicanism. As an alternative to enlightened despotism, benevolent monarchism, republicanism, and rationalism, he took as his goal the improvement of society by means of the cultured individual.[19] He felt that man must be free to pursue those cultural opportunities which would give him a complete personality. The state was to take no active part in this cultural self-education. It was only to encourage and stimulate the happiness of its citizens and see that nothing distracted them while they were seeking cultural advantages.

His belief that the government should refrain from playing a direct part in the life of the citizens put Humboldt in complete opposition to the ideas which Schleiermacher had already expressed on the subject of education. In addition to their diametrically opposed views on the role of the government in the life of the individual, the two men were also in basic disagreement over the possibility of a unified Germany. Humboldt's position on the freedom of the state was an extension of his theory concerning the cultural freedom of the individual, in that he felt that it was as harmful to limit the cultural development of the state as that of the individual. He felt that each German state had distinct characteristics which would be lost or submerged if the states were ever unified in a national German state. He doubted that Germany would be better off politically as a unified state than as a group of strong, separate states, and he emphatically denied that any cultural improvement would result for the German people if unification became a reality.[20]

Feeling as he did that the strength of Germany's traditions lay in separation, and believing as he did that the governments of the separate German states should not interfere directly in the lives of the citizens, Humboldt was naturally opposed to the creation of an educational system under the direct control of the Prussian government. He stated his convictions rather plainly when he said that "national education seems

[19] Reinhold Aris, *A History of Political Thought in Germany from 1789 to 1815*, pp. 137–138.
[20] *Ibid.*, pp. 145, 162; William Humboldt, *The Sphere and Duties of Government*, p. 67.

to me to lie wholly beyond the limits within which a political agency should properly operate."[21]

The contrast between the ideas of Humboldt and Schleiermacher has been discussed in order to show the difficulties Schleiermacher encountered when he worked with Humboldt in trying to reform Prussia's school system. Friedrich still had not learned that naïve sincerity was no substitute for a well-organized program of reform. If a lack of realism prevented the creation of an alliance with Austria and if that same lack of realism caused him to feel disappointment over the unconcern of his congregation at Trinity Church, then Schleiermacher was foolish to think that he could accomplish great feats of nationalism through idealistic educational reforms. Nevertheless, he enthusiastically began his work in 1808 in the section for culture and education, which was under the direction of Humboldt, believing firmly that Prussia could achieve through reforms what she might never have been able to gain by armed uprising against France. If the cautious reforms instituted by Stein could be carried through in fields such as education and government, Prussia could slowly achieve the strength which would be necessary for her to lead a German effort against the French emperor. The main advantage of educational reforms in comparison with military reforms was that they would not being military retaliation by the French.[22]

The section for culture and education in which Schleiermacher hopefully began his work for the regeneration of Prussia had a rather complicated structure. As head of the section Humboldt was responsible to Altenstein, of the Ministry of the Interior. The section for culture and education was divided into the subsection on public instruction, which was also under the direction of Humboldt, and a subsection on culture, the responsibility for which was given to Nicolovius. These two subsections were, in turn, divided into committees, and it was to one of the committees in the subsection on education that Schleiermacher was appointed in 1808. He was later given a similar position in the subsection on culture.[23]

The friction which was bound to occur between Humboldt and Schleiermacher because of their divergent beliefs became most noticeable when the section on education tried to establish some fundamental

[21] Humboldt, *Sphere and Duties of Government,* p. 71.
[22] Schleiermacher to Henrietta von Willich from Berlin, December 15, 1808, Reimer (ed.), *Aus Schleiermachers Leben,* II, 180–181.
[23] Franz Schnabel, *Deutsche Geschichte im neunzehnten Jahrhundert,* I, 455; Seeley, *Life and Times of Stein,* II, 425–427.

guidelines for reforming Prussia's educational system. Humboldt felt that the best method for teaching Prussia's youth would be to minimize the mastery of facts and concentrate upon providing a broad, cultural background. The weakness of the old system of studying the classics and memorizing data was that rote memory drills did not increase the student's power of comprehension. According to Humboldt, students must be motivated to want to learn instead of being forced to reproduce facts, and only a cultural approach to education would produce an incentive strong enough to motivate the students. Humboldt's deliberate omission in his writings of any reference to the needs for instilling devotion and loyalty to the Prussian state or German traditions was perfectly consistent with his avowed dislike for anything nationalistic in nature. What alarmed Schleiermacher was Humboldt's demand that the section on education accept his view as its official philosophy. The fact that Humboldt was so obviously hostile to the use of education as a stimulus for patriotism convinced Friedrich that Humboldt was deliberately violating Stein's intentions for which the section on education and culture had been created. Stein had seen the need for an educational system in Prussia which would prevent another complete collapse of morale like that of 1806. Inculcating Prussian chauvinism in Prussia's youth by glorifying the great deeds of the past would have to be a fundamental part of the educational system. If Humboldt's philosophy was accepted in preference to that of Stein, then in a very real sense Stein's reform efforts would be doomed.

The concern which Schleiermacher felt over the threat to Stein's general reform program because of Humboldt's educational theories led Schleiermacher to examine critically his own views of Prussian education. Ever since 1799 he had been of the opinion that patriotism could be instilled in students by praising the past glories of Prussia, but Humboldt's strong opposition to such a procedure helped Friedrich see that there might not be any such thing as Prussian history and Prussian traditions. After all, so little of what constituted Prussian history was uniquely Prussian that one could hardly use these facts as evidence of the need for loyalty to the Prussian states. If taken to their logical conclusion, facts and events from out of Prussia's past tended to magnify Germany instead of Prussia, and their use would build loyalty to all of Germany, not to just one state. Schleiermacher's belief that Prussia should use her German heritage as a means for establishing Prussian leadership over the rest of Germany began to take on the appearance of an illogical compromise between Humboldt's type of particularism and unlimited German nationalism. A feeling of crisis was created in Schleiermacher's mind by his inability to reject Prussian particularism for this more logical German nationalism, even though he could see that his own adherence to the idea of using German nationalism to further Prussian goals was untenable. The main obstacle in his path toward becoming a nationalist was his attempt to "use" nationalism for the benefit of a nonnationalistic purpose. A man does not become a nationalist until he is conscious of a nationality and makes it the prime object of his patriotism. Loyalty to one's nationality may be conditioned by a great many factors, but somewhere in the process of glorifying national characteristics, one must rise above the level of utility. When one ceases to look upon the blessings of common language, traditions, and cultural patterns as though these were mere historical accidents and begins to feel an emotional patriotism because of them—this is nationalism.[24] That he was satisfied with using nationalistic patriotism for his own particularist purposes in Prussia clearly revealed that Schleiermacher was not quite ready to work for a nationalistic cause like the unification of Germany and nothing could have revealed the inadequacies of his particularism as Humboldt's opposition did.

When one is aware of the deep concern which Schleiermacher had about the tendency of Prussian leaders like Humboldt to undermine Stein's reform program, he can easily imagine the dismay that overcame Schleiermacher when Stein was dismissed from the Prussian government and forced into exile in December, 1808. Napoleon had learned of his efforts to create an alliance against him and had forced Friedrich Wilhelm to have the reformer dismissed. For Schleiermacher the action taken by the King of Prussia against his chief minister meant the end of any hope for success for the reform program in Prussia. Under the spell of gloom which he felt over Stein's departure he wrote his fiancée a letter in which he predicted that the possibility for Prussia to exert strong leadership over Germany had been dealt a severe blow by the King's action. As Schleiermacher interpreted Stein's dismissal the action meant that the great Prussian traditions which Stein had strived to preserve would be lost and the proposed reforms would be dropped. Without great reforms Prussia would never regain her lost prestige, and without strong Prussian leadership Germany would never be free from the tyranny of men like Napoleon. Prussia's great traditions would have placed the country in an excellent position to lift the level of all of Germany, but

[24] Hayes, *Nationalism: A Religion,* pp. 9–10.

these traditions would now be only an interesting object of study from the viewpoint of past history.[25]

The only consolation that Schleiermacher could find while he was experiencing the pangs of defeat over Stein's dismissal was the messianic faith he had in the German people. He knew that there was a possibility that times would become even more difficult for Prussia and the German people than they were in December, 1808, although he could not readily visualize what other unpleasantry could befall his people. Even if the very worst fate should befall Germany, however, he still believed that the German people would continue to be an instrument in the hand of God. God would never allow Germany to be destroyed, proclaimed the young preacher who was soon to become one of Prussia's strongest German nationalists, because the Germans, like the Children of Israel, were a people whom God had set apart for a unique destiny.[26]

A good example of his determination to continue serving Prussia in spite of his discouragement over the King's action against Stein can be seen in the tribute which Friedrich paid to Stein after he left Berlin. Schleiermacher expressed genuine sorrow over the great reformer's fate but he did not grieve over the fact that Stein had been called upon to make a great sacrifice for Prussia. As far as he was concerned, Stein was to be congratulated, for "being declared an enemy of the great nation, France, is the greatest achievement and honor which can befall a person who administers a public office in our day."[27] If he were to experience the same persecutions which Stein had, he would consider this at least a slight indication that he had served as selflessly as the Baron had.

The big question in Schleiermacher's life at the beginning of the year 1809 was in what area he should continue to work for the regeneration of Prussia. Everything in which he had placed hope up to that time had failed. Risking his life on missions as a diplomatic courier, preaching to complacent or indifferent congregations, working for reforms which would make Prussia strong, only to see the reforms lose their momentum —all these had been tried by Schleiermacher with no results of any kind

[25] Schleiermacher to Henrietta von Willich from Berlin, December 15, 1808, Reimer (ed.), Aus Schleiermachers Leben, II, 182–183.
[26] Schleiermacher to Henrietta von Willich from Berlin, December 31, 1808, ibid., II, 195–196.
[27] Schleiermacher to Henrietta von Willich from Berlin, January 26, 1809, ibid., II, 210–211.

84 FRIEDRICH SCHLEIERMACHER

to show that Prussia was better off than when he had begun. Almost from sheer desperation he turned his attention to one last alternative which had not been used in the struggle to help Prussia regain her strength: the creation of a state university which could centralize and focalize patriotic feeling in Prussia.

When Halle and the university there were lost to the French by the Treaty of Tilsit in July, 1807, various Prussian officials immediately began to make plans to replace the University of Halle with another institution. Although the government did not move to establish a school immediately, the need to keep Halle's faculty intact was recognized, and the king accordingly issued an order to cabinet on September 4, 1807, setting aside the funds which had been going to Halle. From these diverted funds the faculty was to be compensated until the government could create a new university.[28] The question of the type and location of the university to be established, coming as it did as part of the general problem of educational reforms in Prussia, was turned over to the section on education and culture in which Schleiermacher was working.

Friedrich had been deeply interested in the possibility of a new university both because of the fact that he was a member of the Halle faculty which would be utilized in the new school and also because as a member of the subsection on education he could see tremendous possibilities for the good of Prussian patriotism in a new institution. As a result of this interest and as part of his official responsibility as a member of the subsection on education, Schleiermacher wrote a very lengthy pamphlet entitled *Random Thoughts concerning Universities in the German Sense: Also a Supplement concerning a New University To Be Established,* in which he described the vital part which the state must play in the creation of any new educational institution in Germany.

As far as Schleiermacher's educational theories were concerned this pamphlet was just a summarization of what he had said on previous occasions, but with regard to his nationalism it showed that he was on the verge of reasoning himself out of his particularism and into German nationalism. In fact, the theme of the pamphlet could easily be said to be the need for instilling patriotism in all German youth by means of a Prussian university.[29] Visualizing an educational institution to benefit all of Germany and not just the narrow confines of Prussia, he scoffed at

[28] Seeley, *The Life and Times of Stein,* II, 431–432.
[29] "Gelegentliche Gedanken über Universitäten im deutschen Sinn, Nebst einem Anhang über eine neu zu errichtande," in Schleiermacher, *Sämmtliche Werke, Zur Philosophie,* I, 539–542.

the notion that the Prussian state would dominate the proposed university if it was located in Berlin and heaped a like amount of scorn upon
the objection that the school would exercise undue influence upon the
Prussian government. He could see only the possibility of service and
cooperation between the Prussian state and the university, not domination by either over the other. Significantly, he pointed out that perhaps
the greatest threat to the success of the proposed university would be the
limiting influence of particularism. This appears to be the first place in
Schleiermacher's many writings where he actually concedes the point
that particularism was directly in opposition to nationalism, for he
stressed the point that the petty fears of biased or uninformed people
were the chief obstacles to progress in Germany.[30]

To be sure, Friedrich was expressing himself about the very limited
subject of a proposed university, but he nevertheless was firmly convinced that Prussian particularism and German nationalism were anti-
thetical. He confessed that he was aware of the petty fears of the Catholic states concerning the importation of "dangerous" ideas from neigh-
boring Protestant universities. He also conceded that there was danger
that one of the larger states, like Prussia, might try to exercise authority
over the smaller ones. He could not help admitting that fears and differences over designs for power by Prussia—designs which he himself had
supported as the answer to the problems of all of Germany—were a
major cause for German disunity. The key to the alleviation of these
fears lay in the creation of institutions like the type of university which
Schleiermacher was advocating for Berlin. Even though the German
states might be different with respect to religion, political outlook, and
economic structure, they all had something in common: the German
language.

A central university would draw people together from all of Germany
and force them to use their common language in scholarly pursuits where
their particularist loyalties would not be compromised. Just being together in the school would have the effect of minimizing the differences
between the states and emphasizing the common cultural traits of all
German people. Catholics and Protestants, Prussians and Hessians, rich
and poor, all would come to see their common destiny and political
potentialities by studying courses together which had nothing to do with
political or religious subject matter. Since Germany's fears were as outdated and unrealistic as her educational systems, alteration and modern-

[30] *Ibid.*, I, 545–552.

ization of the educational methods with the creation of a central university would be a crucial step in ending the differences between a people who belonged together.[31]

Published as it was before Stein's dismissal, this pamphlet reflected much of the optimism that Schleiermacher exhibited in 1808 toward the general progress of reforms in Prussia. It must be noted, however, that his plea for less particularism and more nationalism in education was not duplicated in his attitude toward the political future of Germany, for in spite of his nationalistic appeal in his pamphlet on the proposed Prussian university he still seemed convinced that Prussia should lead the rest of Germany, and eventually would. Then when Stein was forced to leave Prussia and Friedrich experienced a profound disillusionment over the apparent failure of the reform movement, the possibility of creating a bastion of strength for Prussia in the form of a state university became Schleiermacher's last hope. If this failed, then Prussia and all of Germany were doomed.[32] Gone was his optimism as well as his belief that he or anyone else in Prussia could bring about a quick change in Prussia's position of subservience to France.

Schleiermacher's sense of desperation helps explain why he devoted so much of his time and efforts to the erection of the University of Berlin, which was created in 1809 and began its first session in 1810. On the verge of rejecting his loyalty for Prussia and calling for a national German uprising against France for the sake of a unified German nation, he continued to work for the regeneration of Prussia with the slim hope that the impossible would be achieved because of the new center of learning.

The most important series of meetings dealing with the founding of the University of Berlin took place at Humboldt's home in April, 1809, when Humboldt, Fichte, Uhden, Nicolovius, and Schleiermacher met to decide upon the fundamental aims and philosophy of the new school.[33] As had been the case ever since Humboldt and Schleiermacher began working together, the two men disagreed completely on what the underlying philosophy of the Berlin school should be. Humboldt still favored a type of curriculum which was centered in the liberal arts. In trying to

[31] *Ibid.,* I, 547, 563–565.
[32] Schleiermacher to Henrietta von Willich from Berlin, February 12, 1809, Reimer (ed.), *Aus Schleiermachers Leben,* II, 219–220.
[33] "Der Berliner Universitätsplan" in Johann G. Fichte, *Fichtes Leben und literarischer Briefwechsel,* I, 415–416; Schleiermacher to Henrietta von Willich from Berlin, April 10, 1809, Reimer (ed.), *Aus Schleiermachers Leben,* II, 238–239.

equip the student to serve society Humboldt wanted neither help nor interference from the Prussian government. Conversely, Schleiermacher favored a general education in the arts and sciences with the state supervising the school. He continued to insist that since the educational process should be designed to prepare the student to honor and serve the state the state should be allowed to direct the preparation of the material taught in the classrooms. Both men wanted to preserve the old standards of student life and faculty training on a corporate basis, while adding to these standards the legal equality and personal freedom which were fundamental in Stein's plan for general reforms in the Prussian government.[34]

The impasse between Humboldt and Schleiermacher resulted in both men seeing their views materialize in the new University. Schleiermacher convinced the other members of the committee that the school should be very closely supervised by the Prussian government, while Humboldt won his point that an atmosphere of intellectual inquiry should prevail at the institution. Since the founding of the University of Berlin, German universities have borne the imprint of the influence of both these scholars.[35] Aside from this one compromise Schleiermacher's ideas concerning the University of Berlin were generally rejected. The King gave royal sanction to the training schools for teachers which Humboldt established in line with his philosophy of education.[36] Even the Prussian *gymnasien* were reorganized along Humboldt's prescribed lines of cultural orientation.

Schleiermacher also experienced sharp disappointment in his hopes for the complete separation of Church and state educational activities. He had believed that the creation of the University of Berlin would cause the state to take a less active role in Church affairs in Prussia. Instead of less control, the state exercised even more than before, especially in the supervision of the normal schools operated by the Church. To make matters worse the state did not actually assume the financial responsibility which Schleiermacher had felt it should. Financial responsibility for the schools was left in the hands of local deputations in Prussia until early in the twentieth century.[37]

Thus Schleiermacher had seen every one of his educational theories

[34] Schnabel, *Deutsche Geschichte,* I, 449.
[35] *Ibid.,* I, 445; Theobald Ziegler, *Die geistigen und sozialen Strömungen des neunzehnten Jahrhunderts,* pp. 97–98.
[36] Seeley, *The Life and Times of Stein,* II, 429–430.
[37] Thomas Alexander, *The Prussian Elementary School,* pp. 36–38.

rejected wholly or in part by the time the University of Berlin began its first session in 1810. The joy that he should have felt when he was appointed to head the Department of Theology at the University was turned into fatalistic resignation because he felt that the school which was part of his own creation was a failure before classes ever started. He knew that the University could have been a powerful force in arousing the patriotism of its students, but he also knew that this would never happen because those who administered the school were opposed to the use of the classes for nationalistic purposes.

The frustration of total defeat which Schleiermacher felt in 1810 due to the failure of all his efforts to create and stimulate patriotic sentiment in Prussia was summed up well by him in a sermon which he preached late in that year entitled "When the Lord Could Say with Truth That He Had Finished."[38] The title of the sermon was drawn from the dying words of Jesus as He was hanging on the cross. Friedrich made note of the fact that a life given in sacrifice for others is not a lost life, but is a life more filled with meaning than is a saved life with no purpose. The death of Jesus had meaning only because His life had had meaning.[39] Rather bitterly Schleiermacher asked if the people of Prussia would ever be able to say that their life had been one of meaning. Of course all of the people would experience death after having made some impact upon society, but Schleiermacher felt that man should approach the time of death knowing that he had accomplished something worthwhile, or at least that he had tried to accomplish something. The real victory would be in striving for good, not necessarily in achieving it.[40]

The only consolation for Friedrich Schleiermacher in 1810 was that he had tried his best to give dedicated service to Prussia. He had worked on the premise that if Prussia regained her strength she could assert leadership over the rest of the German states, who would rally to the Prussian flag and drive France from Germany. Then in some vague manner, which Schleiermacher had not thought through completely, Prussia would use the German nationalism, to which she had appealed for help against the French, to create a German nation over which she would exercise control. Now, four years after he had seen a vision of Prussia's rebirth, Schleiermacher could find no visible signs that his country would ever be able to lead Germany in any kind of national

<hr />

[38] "Wie der Herr mit Recht sagen konnte, das er vollbrachte habe," in Schleiermacher, *Sämmtliche Werke, Predigten,* VII, 383–390.

[39] *Ibid.,* VII, 383–384.

[40] *Ibid.,* VII, 385–386.

movement. Time and again, in appealing to Prussian particularism, Schleiermacher had almost admitted that nationalism, not particularism, was the only solution to Germany's problems. However, he did not abandon his hope for Prussian patriotism until he finally became convinced of the utter and complete patriotic depravity of the Prussian people.

Boyd Shafer has maintained in his *Nationalism: Myth and Reality* that the necessary ingredients for nationalism can be neither given to a man nor forced upon him. A feeling like patriotism springs forth in a man when events have prepared him for it.[1] What Shafer held as true of nationalism in general could certainly be said of Schleiermacher in particular in 1811. By that year Schleiermacher had been sufficiently conditioned by events in his life to make the transition from Prussian patriotism to German nationalism. He realized that a national awakening in Germany would be the only hope for both his native Prussia and his German homeland. This conclusion, which came as a result of an agonizing reappraisal of his country's role as a European power, was the final development in a long series of logical steps which he had taken over a period of twenty-five years. Had it not been for the disillusionment he felt in 1811 over the inability of Prussia to lift herself out of her state of indifference, all the earlier seemingly unconnected phases of his life might have counted for nothing as far as his nationalism was concerned. In retrospect each separate segment of his intellectual, religious, social, and political life seemed to be a preparatory step toward the day when he would look upon a national German movement as the answer to the needs of all of Germany.

As the Pietist, Schleiermacher had acquired a deep sense of reverence for the unseen, the idealistic, the theoretical. When he broke all his ties with the Moravian Brethren at Barby to study rationalism, he retained his reverence for the mystical and sentimental aspects of the Pietists. This reverence in itself did not make him a nationalist but it did give him the emotional foundation upon which the spirit of nationalism so often was built. His intensive study of rationalistic Kantian ethics, coming as it did immediately after his Pietistic experiences, led him to see the value of practical political concepts when they were used in conjunction with a

[1] Boyd Shafer, *Nationalism: Myth and Reality*, p. 146.

sense of spiritual guidance. Rationalism taught him to fear unbridled reason as much as Pietism had led him to fear uncontrolled emotionalism. As in the case of Pietism, rationalism did not immediately turn Schleiermacher into a determined nationalist. It merely prepared him for the day when he would rationally apply the sense of devotion he felt for his homeland to all of Germany. He did not begin to express openly a nationalistic viewpoint until after he had completed his studies of rationalism and had begun to associate with the romanticists. As a consequence of his contacts with these impractical dreamers he learned that he could apply Pietistic emotionalism and rationalistic logic to studies of antiquity. He was attracted to the romanticists' love for folk language and their compassion for philological studies. He came to share their wide interest in folk history, which opened a whole new world of interpretation in the areas of jurisprudence and comparative religion.[2] The experiences which he had in the Berlin circle of romanticists made nationalism a process that was not only possible for him, but perhaps irresistible.[3] Schleiermacher had gently been exposed to the kernel of truth which every nationalist must come to accept: a man must love his nation's past. The combined interactions of Pietism, rationalism, and romanticism led him along a course toward which none of the three, acting independently, would have directed him. Any of the three could have given to Schleiermacher the breadth of vision which would have enabled him to apply this newly learned principle to the whole of Germany. The interworking of these integrated forces, however, merely brought him to the state of mind where his supreme loyalty was directed to the state. His mistake was in limiting the interpretation of what constituted a true nation to the territory ruled by Prussia.

Schleiermacher still had a long way to go before he could make the transition to a real feeling of nationalism covering the whole of Germany. Even though he prided himself on his German language and customs, from 1795 until 1806 he gave practically no indication that he was in any way concerned for the fate of the German territories under the domination of France. Even after the Tilsit agreements between France and Russia by which Prussia was so drastically reduced in size and population his only interest in the other German states was in the assistance which they might give to Prussia in her struggle to drive out the French. He was aware of the fact that only a united effort against France by the German people could rid Prussia of the yoke of French oppression, but this did

---

[2] Carlton J. H. Hayes, *Essays on Nationalism*, p. 54.
[3] *Ibid.*, p. 59.

not mean that as a result of a victory over the French the German people should have a unified nation. When he spoke of a unified Germany he meant only an expanded or enlarged Prussian state. The reforms which he advocated in education were reforms only for Prussian schools although he grudgingly admitted that the principle behind them would be as practical for other states as for Prussia. In the process of looking for a common denominator upon which the Prussian government could build a feeling of Prussian patriotism he advanced a proposal which ultimately led him from Prussian to German nationalism. Believing, like Johann Gottlieb Herder, that the German language could become the key factor in Prussian patriotism without leading to German unification, he wanted to build a state university where the use of the German language would serve as a rallying point for a Prussian spirit.[4] When the University of Berlin came into being in the fall of 1810 he believed that at last Prussia had an institution which would produce a patriotic pro-Prussian generation of young people. Thus he was still thinking in terms of Prussian particularism as late as 1810.

After he taught at the University of Berlin for a year Schleiermacher knew that he had ben entirely wrong about Prussian patriotism. This admission came partly as a result of the failure of the University of Berlin to become a stimulant for Prussian state loyalty and partly as a consequence of his first clear insight into the nature of Prussia's basic problems. These realizations threw him into a state of despair which caused him to re-evaluate Prussia as a part of Germany instead of as a separate nation. Once he had properly related his feelings for Prussia to all of Germany his despair turned to determination. Shortly thereafter the War of Liberation presented Germany with what Schleiermacher considered to be its greatest opportunity to create from chaos and indecision a nation of German people.

Schleiermacher began voicing his complaints over the failure of the University of Berlin to live up to its patriotic potentialities only a few months after the University commenced its first year of instruction. His hopes that the new state institution would prove to be a revitalizing factor in Prussian patriotism had not materialized in spite of the fact that he and many others like him had striven for a patriotic atmosphere in the school. In view of the potentialities and the personal dedication of the faculty he felt that he had every right to be disappointed with the meager service rendered to Prussia by the University.

---

[4] Hans Kohn, *Nationalism: Its Meaning and History*, p. 9; Robert Ergang, *Herder and the Foundations of German Nationalism*, pp. 246–247.

In a letter to a friend in September, 1811, Schleiermacher tried to ascertain the source of failure of the new school. He turned his attention first to the members of the faculty and administration who feared the French. These "despicable people," who harbored an obsessive fear that any patriotic utterance would bring the wrath of France down upon Prussia, had consciously blocked any move to orientate the University of Berlin's curriculum around a nationalistic approach. A group with even more influence than those who feared the French actually welcomed French intervention in Prussian affairs. Schleiermacher was not sure whether it would be worse to be a coward or a traitor, but he insisted that Prussia had room for neither in her University. Prussia would never arrive at a place where she would be able to throw off the humiliation of French hegemony if the repository of Prussian intellectual activity cried for nothing but "peace! peace! peace!" Schleiermacher recounted to his friend the joys that should have come to a professor who had wanted to serve as an educator as much as Schleiermacher had. The satisfaction which he had anticipated had simply eluded him. Schleiermacher asked his friend how could there be joy in the heart of a man who saw his institution in the hands of those who were pacifistic or naïve.[5]

Having said this much Schleiermacher expanded his criticism to include the Prussian government. The French had presented Prussia with a rare opportunity for the growth of the spirit of patriotism by breathing into the breasts of Prussians a zeal for freedom, he reasoned. Instead of tapping this spirit, he lamented, the government had succeeded in killing it with antiquated education policies. Any good German would have wanted to see the University of Berlin stand as a beacon of hope for a new day in Prussia. If the government, with its lack of patriotism, and the University's staff and faculty, with their lack of insight, caused the University of Berlin to fail as a national institution, then there could be no hope for Prussian particularism.[6]

For the first time in his life Schleiermacher experienced what he could well have called his moment of truth. Prussia was not a nation. It was only a collection of people under the leadership of a king. The necessary ingredients which would turn the Prussian people into a nation were not present and they never would be. The government, the people, and the educated leadership were all unfit for the task of creating a strong

[5] Schleiermacher to Johannes Schulze from Berlin, September 13, 1811, Heinrich Meisner (ed.), *Schleiermacher als Mensch: Sein Werden und Wirken, Familien—und Freundesbriefe*, II, 138–139.

[6] *Ibid.*, II, 139.

nationalistic state out of Prussia. He now understood why the use of the German language in the University of Berlin had failed to stimulate a spirit of Prussian nationalism. The German language could be used successfully only to stimulate a spirit of German nationalism.

The grim reality of seeing Prussia in its true light for the first time rendered Schleiermacher temporarily incapable of action. It was a severe blow for him to realize that all his sacrifices for the sake of Prussia since 1806 had been in vain, and he endured some of the worst mental trials of his entire life during the month of September, 1811, while he sought to replace his old goals with valid ones. However, in a letter to a relative late in that month he showed that he had emerged from his inner struggle with the firm resolution that there could be only one remedy for the troubles of Prussia and Germany: all of Germany must immediately forget the differences which had kept the states apart for centuries, and in the place of these differences there must be a genuine feeling of comradeship built on the foundation of a common cultural and linguistic heritage. He suggested that in the transition from particularism to nationalism only that which was common to all Germans should be retained. Henceforth only acts which would contribute to the unification of the German people would be worthy of the time of Prussians, Hanovarians, Hessians, and Pomeranians. For the sake of each other the citizens of all the German territories must become reconciled to destruction and devastation, for unification would have to be a bloody, but commonly shared, act of suffering. This would mean that Prussians would have to suffer for Bavarians and the Pomeranians for the Anhalters—a phenomenon never before experienced in Germany because each group of Germans had always acted in the interest of its own welfare. Schleiermacher said that the time had come for all Germans to realize that they could act in their own best interests only by considering the welfare of all of Germany. Germans must rise above their narrow particularism for in Schleiermacher's opinion no lesser effort could merit the reward of freedom and unity.[7]

Not many months before he had written this letter Schleiermacher himself had pleaded for the continued emphasis of particularistic interpretations in the field of education, feeling at the time that the various German states would be wise to avoid any type of educational approach

[7] Schleiermacher to Charlotte von Kathen from Berlin, September [14], 1811, Georg Reimer (ed.), *Aus Schleiermachers Leben in Briefen,* II, 252–253.

which would hamper or detract from particularist loyalties.[8] Now Schleiermacher predicted that the German people would have to be satisfied with the curse of particularism unless they were willing to endure the hard times required to achieve something better.[9] The spirit of nationalism is often bound by conflicting loyalties like the particularist feelings of the German people. The elimination of these restrictions so that the individual can focus his attention upon the supreme goal for the good of the nation is the major achievement of the nationalist.[10] In September, 1811, Schleiermacher succeeded in rising above the restrictive elements of his nationalistic viewpoint.

Schleiermacher was able to make a smooth transition from Prussian particularism to German nationalism because his Prussian patriotism had been flexible. This allowed him to enlarge his viewpoint and expand his sense of patriotism without destroying either his patriotism or his nationalism.[11] In the process of altering his nationalism Schleiermacher was also able to acquire a new virtue: he learned to be patient. Before 1811 he acted under a sense of urgency, which constantly led him into activities of a risky and fruitless nature. After he recognized the true nature of German nationalism he was able to wait patiently for the time when historical circumstances in favor of Germany would lead all of the German people to join hands in one nation. Except for one letter, which hinted about a trip which he had taken for political purposes in 1811,[12] Schleiermacher left no evidence that he was involved in any secret activity such as serving as a diplomatic courier for the patriotic clubs in Berlin in 1811 and 1812. It would not be an exaggeration to say that even his attitude toward his service to Prussia underwent a change when his interpretation of nationalism changed. Whereas he had once derived a great deal of personal satisfaction from his duties in the Ministry of the Interior he now concluded that his efforts on behalf of limited Prussian programs of education were a waste of his time.[13] The restlessness

[8] "Gelegentliche Gedanken über Universitäten im deutschen Sinn," Nebst einem Anhang über eine neu zu errichtande, in Friedrich Schleiermacher, *Sämmtliche Werke, Zur Philosophie*, I, 539–565.

[9] Schleiermacher to Charlotte von Kathen from Berlin, September [14], 1811, Reimer (ed.), *Aus Schleiermachers Leben*, II, 252–253.

[10] Carlton J. H. Hayes, *Nationalism: A Religion*, p. 10.

[11] Leonard Krieger, *The German Idea of Freedom*, pp. 177–178.

[12] Henrietta Schleiermacher to Schleiermarcher from Berlin [September 1811], Reimer (ed.), *Aus Schleiermachers Leben*, II, 253.

[13] Schleiermacher to Karl Gustaf von Brinckmann from Berlin, July 4, 1812, Meisner (ed.), *Schleiermacher als Mensch*, II, 147.

which he experienced in a service that once had been so highly valued by him signified that purely Prussian nationalism was a dead issue for him. He decided that until Germany could rid herself of the blight of sectionalism and particularism he would spend his time studying the Greek philosophers, lecturing to the students of the University of Berlin, and writing papers for presentation before the Royal Academy of Berlin.[14]

While Schleiermacher taught, worked, and waited, the events which were to give his fellow Germans the chance to fight for their freedom slowly started to unfold. The shaky alliance which had been created between France and Russia in 1807 started to deteriorate almost as soon as it had been consummated. At the very time when Schleiermacher complained of the lack of an issue around which to rally the German people Napoleon was preparing for a war against his ally to the east. War was a reality when the French emperor led an army of 600,000 men across the Niemen River on June 24, 1812. His advance was uninterrupted until the month of September when he stood before the deserted city of Moscow. The absence of a decisive victory in the field was made more unbearable by the disastrous retreat of Napoleon's army, which cost him four-fifths of the forces which he had taken into Russia. By December, 1812, these haggard forces began to straggle into Prussia. The sight of the shattered remnants of the Napoleonic armies convinced men like General Yorck, in command of the only Prussian army, that the time had come for Prussia to turn against France. In December, 1812, Yorck arranged with the Russians the Convention of Tauroggen, in which he agreed to keep the forces of Prussia neutral until he received further instructions from King Friedrich Wilhelm III. Even if the King should order the Prussian troops to renew their conflict with Russian troops Yorck promised that he would not resume fighting until February, 1813. By the time that Yorck was to begin fighting again Stein had returned from exile in Russia and was encouraging a national uprising against the French. The possibility grew greater each day that the King would change sides, call out the *Landwehr,* and begin a crusade to liberate Prussia.

Under the spell of the excitement aroused by the events of December, 1812, Schleiermacher made a mistake in judgment which was to plague him for several months. He assumed that there would be an immediate demonstration of German nationalism because of the weakness of the

[14] *Ibid.*

French army. He thought that the mobilization of the Prussian army would symbolize the beginning of a general German effort to unify all the German states. He had no way of knowing that as soon as the Prussian army was no longer needed for Prussia's defense the country's leadership would revert to its old narrow point of view without any regard for the hopes which German nationalists might have for a national German state.

On January 2, 1813, when the full impact of the defeat of Napoleon's army became evident Schleiermacher wrote to Alexander zu Dohna expressing the fear that the time for determined action was quickly slipping away from Germany. He maintained that there would be absolutely no hope for success against France if Prussia continued her policy of pitiful passivity and inactivity.[15] Schleiermacher was at that time unaware that the King was working on means and methods whereby the Prussian and Russian forces might be joined in an effort against France. All he knew was that Prussian troops were being used against Russian forces when they should have been fighting with the Russian armies against the French. He saw that any hope for a national awakening would depend upon a successful war against France and that this war was out of the question as long as the king maintained his alliance with Napoleon. He had no great love for Russia or for the Czar, who had helped humiliate Prussia at Tilsit and would probably do it again if the opportunity arose; however, in spite of the great dislike which he felt for the past actions of the Russians, as a nationalist the only matter worthy of consideration for him was the freedom of Germany. If Russia could help Germany achieve her longed-for unity, then personal animosities would have to take a temporary position of lesser importance. All of Schleiermacher's hopes and dreams were predicated upon the assumption that given the proper set of circumstances Prussia would rise above her past and lead the German people in a war of national liberation. If in spite of opportunities to break off relations with Napoleon and join hands with Russia the royal court continued its policy of sacrificing Prussian soldiers in alliance with France, then Prussia would forfeit her right to become a part of a united Germany.

Schleiermacher pointed out to Alexander that Prussia was already paying a terrible price for her willingness to cooperate with France. The remnants of the contingents of the Prussian army which had been fool-

[15] Schleiermacher to Alexander zu Dohna from Berlin, January 2, 1813, Meisner (ed.), *Schleiermacher als Mensch*, II, 147.

ishly sent with Napoleon into Russia were beginning to return home. He was hurt to see that these men were little more than slackers and deserters, who had been forced to fight for a cause in which they did not believe. The worst was yet to come, for unless the energies of these men were directed against the French they would become vagabonds and common criminals once the military authority over them was relaxed. The day would soon come when the people of Prussia would hope for a force of fully equipped police to protect them from their own army.[16] Schleiermacher said that when he visualized the potentialities of the Prussian army and then compared this mental image with what the Prussian army was actually doing, he wanted to cry. What would it take to transform the army of deserters and disheartened quitters into a true fighting force? He unhesitatingly answered his own question by saying that only a campaign for the redemption of the German nationality would bring out the inherent gifts of the Prussian soldier.

The Berlin theologian was so convinced that Prussia was playing the part of the fool that he invoked the curse of God upon those who would not recognize the course Prussia must take in leading Germany into a national unification movement. He demonstrated once again the unique interaction of religious and patriotic influences upon the viewpoint of the nationalist by charging those who shirked their national responsibilities with blasphemy. To be sure, noted Schleiermacher, the innocent might suffer from the devastation which a war of national liberation might bring to Prussia but those who purposely frustrated nationalistic efforts must ultimately answer to God for their crime and neglect. This *fiat justitia, pereat mundus* was the principle which enabled him to endure the heartaches he felt during the days just before and during the War of Liberation. Since the cause of nationalism was blessed of God, as long as Prussia existed, there was room for hope that a national movement would succeed. Schleiermacher vowed that he would preach the unification of Germany to the people of his congregation and teach it to the students in his classes at the University until the victory had been won or until Germany had been so thoroughly crushed that the German cause would die of betrayal.[17]

Schleiermacher did not have to wait long for dramatic events to change the course of German history. By the middle of March, 1813, Prussia and Russia had signed the Treaty of Breslau, the terms of which

[16] *Ibid.*, II, 147.
[17] *Ibid.*, II, 147–148.

required Prussia to contribute eighty thousand troops to be used against France. In return for these soldiers the Russians agreed to restore and enlarge Prussia's pre-Napoleonic territory. The War of Liberation had begun. Friedrich Schleiermacher, feeling that the greatest moment in Germany's history had come to pass, was enraptured.

Filled with the conviction that his Prussia had finally arrived at the point in history where, with proper leadership and devotion, she could lead the German people in a truly national war effort, the Berlin preacher delivered in the first month of the War what must be considered one of the greatest national sermons ever preached. No other document so clearly reveals the depth of devotion which he had developed for the yet unborn German national state; nor does any other single instance from the story of his life reveal the completeness of his concentration upon arousing Prussian people to a nationalistic uprising. In the opening words of the sermon he equated the reversal of the fortunes of the French armies with an act of divine intervention. He recalled the joy the Berliners had felt when their "allies," the French, had fled the city and the "enemy," the Russians, had entered. But the joy expressed over the departure of the French and the entrance of the Russians had been nothing compared to the rejoicing over the return of the Prussian army, free and ready to fight the French. The defeat of France in Russia and the return of Prussia's army to Berlin had to be considered, according to Schleiermacher, as tokens of the favor which God would continue to show to Germany as the German states fulfilled their national destiny.

The swell of enthusiasm which rocked Berlin was the very thing for which he had prayed for a decade. Unable to contain his enthusiasm he called upon his listeners at the Trinity Church to give God the credit for all that had occurred to the benefit of Prussia "through the fearful turmoil in the North!"[18] This messianic type of interpretation of the conflict of 1812 and 1813 was quite in keeping with the Berlin pastor's nationalistic convictions that his nation was an active instrument in the hands of God. However, he was quick to add that the Lord had had some willing helpers, for the victory thus far had been the result of the efforts of all the people. He interpreted the change in Prussia's military alliance with France as the first truly national German effort by the Prussian people with the population, the military, and the King all contributing. The

---

[18] "A Nation's Duty in a War for Freedom," in Friedrich Schleiermacher, *Selected Sermons of Schleiermacher*, p. 67. Also in condensed form in Timotheus Klein, *Die Befreiung, 1813, 1814, 1815. Urkunden Berichte, Briefe; mit geschichtliche Verbindungen*, p. 155.

military leaders, motivated by bravery and nobility, had turned their guns on the armies which since the Tilsit agreements of 1807 had been the symbol of the humiliation of Prussia's honor. Disregarding the "appearance of disobedience and the infraction of the letter, and acting really according to the mind and spirit of the King," they had "dared to take the first decisive step towards freeing us from the intolerable bonds under which we had so long been held."[19]

Had the War been only the work of the military Schleiermacher would have had little cause for rejoicing, but this had not been the case. The King had remained true to the trust which nationalists like the Trinity pastor had placed in him. He admitted to his congregation that he himself had often despaired of any concerted action by the King, but Friedrich Wilhelm had closed the ranks with a summons to the people to take up arms. From the pastor's point of view this was the act not of a sovereign commanding subjects but of a leader calling upon his fellow men. A new day had dawned upon Prussia and Germany when Schleiermacher had seen his own beloved King come among the people with "a feeling . . . that can never before have lifted up his heart for he never before had an opportunity of feeling so deeply and truly that which is the source of the highest happiness and exaltation to a ruler, the purest harmony between his will and his people's will."[20]

Because of the response of the King and the military to the challenge of the hour, a special responsibility had befallen the citizenry. The preacher knew, as did those who listened to him, that the French had not been defeated simply because they had withdrawn from Berlin. The crucial battles were still to be fought. Germans had observed Napoleon's military genius too long to assume that victory would come easily or cheaply. There was the distinct possibility that France would yet be victorious, but Schleiermacher now considered ultimate victory over France as a secondary matter. The old Prussia could not be defeated for it no longer existed. Its place had been taken by a king and an inspired mass of people who were attempting to create a united German nation. Prussia was no longer a kingdom; it was a spirit. If it cost Prussia her life to find her soul the expense would be none too great. This was the message which Schleiermacher had in mind when he had selected the title for his sermon, "A Nation's Duty in a War for Freedom." The great danger was not that Prussia might be defeated in battle against the French but that even in victory she might lose the precious nationalistic spirit which she

19 Schleiermacher, *Selected Sermons*, pp. 67–68.
20 *Ibid.*, p. 68.

had acquired. This would happen unless the citizens took note of what actually had taken place in their homeland, or, as Schleiermacher stated it, "what in this respect, is the exact significance and the real nature of the change; and second, what we must therefore feel called to do."[21]

Having thus stated the basic changes that had occurred in Prussia because the people had acknowledged their national obligations to the rest of Germany, Schleiermacher proceeded to tell his congregation why Prussia had been humiliated by France in the first place. According to him, in days past, by means of good rulers, judicious decisions, and several successful was, "but mostly through the growing up of a noble and free aspiring spirit in the people themselves, we became a nation and a kingdom regarding which the whole world saw that the Lord would build and plant it and promised to do it good." Then came Prussia's dramatic fall. She had become haughty and proud, living on her reputation instead of on her power. Her whole attitude became perverted. Despondency followed among the people in the wake of the old spirit of self-confidence. Then to the unending discredit of Prussia her "very sense of honor became more and more an empty name. And more and more our heart departed from the Lord."[22] Only a few seemed to notice that the old virtues of Germany had been displaced by vanity and dissipation but no one had been willing to listen to these few who began calling Prussia back to her great traditions of the past. During the time when the nation refused to listen to the nationalistic prophets God had commenced His work of bringing judgment upon the people, using the French armies as an instrument of punishment.

One cannot help noticing the group concepts of guilt that Schleiermacher advanced. As did the Jewish prophets of the Old Testament he pictured the punishment of defeat as a visitation of the wrath of the Lord upon a whole nation, not upon groups of individually sinful people. He maintained almost a deterministic, cause-and-result attitude when he said that as a result of the departure of the Prussians from their traditions "there fell upon us that grievous, crushing disaster in war, and this sudden fall from the height into the abyss was followed by the even more deeply and painfully suicidal calamity of peace."[23]

Schleiermacher made it clear that when he spoke of calamities he was not referring to privation, distress, and poverty. He was speaking of inward spiritual corruption. One must keep in mind, however, that he was

[21] *Ibid.*, p. 69.
[22] *Ibid.*, p. 71.
[23] *Ibid.*, p. 71.

delivering a sermon, not a lecture, and quite naturally he couched his ideas in theological terminology. Even then his listeners must surely have understood that he was focusing attention upon the responsibility of the individual in the fortunes and misfortunes of the nation. After all, a nation could expect only what it deserved from the collective feelings of the whole population. By bearing indignities for seven years because of fear that overt acts would only increase the evil of their day, the people of Prussia had spread, increased, and multiplied their own cowardice and sluggishness. Finally, the sense of being worthy of a better condition was no longer present in the people. The personal lives of Prussia's citizens led to the defeat of the nation, and then the spirit of defeat in the nation came back to haunt the personal relations of the people who had contributed to the defeat. Everyone in Prussia sought to escape from reality through falsehood and fraud. The result was that the Prussians could only despise and detest one another, with no regard for the noble things of life. Though the history of Prussia clearly indicated that the people had once been held together in a bond of unity, that bond and the spirit which motivated it had disappeared, leaving only the selfish individuals who grasped at any sign of luxury they could find. In truth, Prussia was not a nation, noted Schleiermacher.[24]

Having classified himself as one of the few who had sensed the decay of Prussian life during the French occupation, he recalled that he and others had been concerned with the question of whether Prussia's moral fiber had become so weak that a national awakening would be impossible. If she had deteriorated to the level some had claimed, then an armed revolt against France would only drive the weaklings to new low levels of cowardice and depravity. Schleiermacher thanked his God that the doubts concerning military operations against France had been lifted by the winter campaign of the Russians. The return of the Prussian armies was more than a signal for the return of freedom; it evidenced a return to truth.

Schleiermacher continued his great nationalistic exhortation by saying that before the expulsion of the French, men could use the occupation as an excuse for their actions of cowardice. This excuse no longer existed— a fact that Schleiermacher brought to the attention of his listeners. There would no longer be any excuse for lack of patriotism or loyalty. As he expressed it, "Now, thank God, we can again say when we abhor, or

[24] *Ibid.*, pp. 71–72.

when we love and respect; . . . every man of honor must stand to his word
with deeds."[25] When the King helped the Prussian people recover a national will to live he set them on a course of brave acts which could end
in only two ways: glorious ruin or the firm establishment of the blessing
of liberty. Though they had responded with enthusiasm the people must
never lose sight of the goal for which they were fighting. It was not individual people who were participating in the war against France. Rather,
a whole nation was involved in a life-or-death struggle with the final outcome resting with the masses of individuals who constituted Prussia. The
conflict must be based upon the hope that "we shall be able to preserve
for ourselves our own distinctive character, our laws, our constitution and
our culture. Every nation, my dear friends, which had developed a particular, or clearly defined height is degraded also by receiving into it a
foreign element."[26] Thus God had imparted to each its own nature, and
had therefore marked out bounds and limits for the inhabitants of the
different races. Schleiermacher could state his nationalistic feeling no
more strongly than when he argued that God had ordained that the
German people should be free to develop their distinctive character
which had evolved from the cumulated traditions of the past. The boun-
daries for the new German nation were to be established solely on the
basis of the nationality of the German people. All considerations besides
nationality would have to be disregarded immediately and without hesi-
tation. So long as Prussia led Germany in a struggle to establish a nation
on the basis of the national rights which God had ordained, that war
would be a holy war, for "in Him is that nation trusting which means to
defend at any price the distinctive aims and spirit which it has had implanted in it, and is thus fighting for God's work."[27]

How could Schleiermacher be so sure that Prussia would not be fighting for personal gain? How could he be certain that he was actually wit-
nessing the beginning of a new era in Germany with Prussia constituting
only a single element in a vast German movement? He said that many
phenomenal experiences attested to the change in the spirit of Prussia,
which would of course be the source of the spirit of the new Germany.
For instance, here was the willingness on the part of thousands of Prussians to sacrifice their possessions and their lives for a new Germany. The
voluntary spirit of the masses clearly indicated that an old era was dead

[25] *Ibid.*, p. 73.
[26] *Ibid.*, pp. 73–74.
[27] *Ibid.*, p. 74.

and that a new one had been born. An even greater sign of a new day for Germany was the destruction of the wall separating soldiers from citizens. The Prussian military system had been the heart and soul of particularist Prussia. Through the capable leadership of Scharnhorst and Gneisenau, Prussia had created new flexible military units in the *Landwehr*, patterned after the French use of the nation-in-arms, and the *Landsturm*, built upon the idea of holding the young and the aged as a reserve behind the *Landwehr*.

Scharnhorst's plan for rebuilding Prussia's military strength was centered in the *Landwehr* and the *Landsturm*. The *Landwehr* law promulgated by Friedrich Wilhelm called for service in the *Landwehr* of all male citizens between the ages of seventeen and forty. The Prussian districts were to form committees consisting of deputies from the gentry, the towns, and the peasantry. These committees would have the authority to call into service all men of age who were not serving in the regular army. The estates were to select a general to work with an officer selected by the King. The two were to oversee the committee in securing the levies and the necessary equipment. The uniform of the *Landwehr* was very simple and the training was extremely superficial. The ranks of the *Landwehr* were made up mostly of peasants and common laborers, since most of the educated young men joined volunteer units of the regular army. The supplies of arms for the *Landwehr* were so pathetic that Napoleon was said to have laughed at the first contingents with which he came in contact. The *Landsturm* came into being five weeks after the *Landwehr* was created. It was the brainchild of Bartholdi, a civilian official, and was not the work of the military. All male citizens between fifteen and sixty years of age were subject to the call of the *Landsturm*. These units were seldom used in combat, serving rather as a second line of defense behind the *Landwehr*, and performing menial tasks behind the lines. Schleiermacher took a great deal of pride in the *Landsturm* for he served for over a year in a Berlin unit made up of the university professors. With a regular army of trained volunteers, a reserve army of able-bodied citizens, and a second reserve behind both, Prussia would no longer have to depend upon the mercenary armies she had been forced to use. Within the ranks of the new armies the old aristocratic nature of the officer would melt away under the pressure of a common cause. These new military units utilizing the citizen would create a spirit where the only noticeable differences between the officer class and the ranks would be "between those who, constantly occupied with the proper arts of war, are, in the precision of their exercises and performances, an example to all others as well as the nucleus to which they gather, and those who, scantily instructed and drilled, only take up arms when it becomes necessary."[28]

In continuing his lengthy sermon on the role of the nation in a struggle for freedom Schleiermacher recounted the fact that in Prussia's glorious past the fathers had been worthy examples to their sons. The national army now gave the young men of Prussia the opportunity to show the worth of the German youth to their fathers. As far as he was concerned, the real value of the *Landwehr* lay in its symbolism. He did not consider it out of place to read from the Holy Desk of the Church the *Landwehr* summons just issued by Friedrich Wilhelm, for this summons constituted a spiritual as well as a military challenge to the population.[29]

Following the reading of the summons Schleiermacher delivered a word of caution to his congregation. He carefully warned them that there were certain aims that the soldiers and civilians must keep in mind to make the efforts of the *Landwehr* successful. He reminded them that in their acts of bravery the participants in the war against France must think only of the nation. They would have to battle for their homeland and not for personal liberties. He justified this admonition with an analysis of death that showed the vital role which Pietistic mysticism played in shaping his nationalism.[30] He said that when a soldier fights to preserve his personal liberty and dies in the effort his death is a total waste, for he has to live to enjoy the liberty. This meaningless and useless waste of human life could not occur if the soldier fought for his homeland, because death which comes as a result of service for the homeland "must appear to him only as an utterly insignificant casualty, which he must himself regard as little as it can be regarded on the whole."[31]

There can be little doubt that Schleiermacher was speaking about death in abstract terms. He was discussing the loss of life from the viewpoint of the Christian mystic who values death because it unites the soul with God. He certainly recognized that the death of a soldier was a tragedy, irrespective of the circumstances. He was laboring to establish the point that the only meaningful death for a soldier would be for the sake of his country. His attitude toward death for the defense of a national cause was quite in keeping with the general nationalist view that ultimately all other human emotions and loyalties must be subordinated to

[28] Schleiermacher, *Selected Sermons*, p. 75.
[29] *Ibid.*, p. 76; Franz Schnabel, *Deutsche Geschichte im neunzehnten Jahrhundert*, I, 492–493.
[30] Elie Kedourie, *Nationalism*, pp. 86–87.
[31] Schleiermacher, *Selected Sermons*, p. 77.

the good of the nationality.[32] Death in battle would in this sense convey a type of immortality to the man who had loved his country enough to die for it. As a part of the nation the dead soldier would live on after his death because the nation would continue to live. Likwise, the same interpretation should be given to acts of valor as to acts which resulted in death. Just as a true nationalist could not die while the nation continued to exist, so would it also hold true that the nationalist could not merit individual praise for the act of battle bravery. Schleiermacher sincerely believed that for the true citizen "the consciousness of having done all that it was possible for zeal and good will to do, and the recognition of those who know this, outweigh all other distinctions."[33] One must acknowledge that Schleiermacher may have been carried away by his own oratory at this point but even if he did exaggerate a little the point was still obvious.

As the pastor of the Trinity Church drew near the conclusion of this lengthy but extremely revealing sermon on national duties during a war for national freedom, he could see only one possibility for failure in the liberation movement. He was afraid that there might be a tendency to halt the movement toward a nation-in-arms as soon as the French showed signs of defeat. He noted that some who looked upon a further build-up of military forces as a tragic waste were referring to the Prussian advances as a pursuit of "scattered, terrified remnant of the enemy's ruined forces."[34] For anyone to call a halt to the war against France was an indication that he did not understand the basic objectives of the conflict. Prussia was not trying merely to free itself from the oppression of France. Prussia's goal was to liberate Germany from foreign hindrances which might prevent the proper development of the German spirit. To be sure, the armies were no longer in the immediate vicinity of Berlin, but these distant armies which were pressing hard upon the retreating French were no longer mercenaries who could be easily forgotten. The Prussian armies were made up of fathers, brothers, sons, and husbands, as well as benefactors, close friends, pupils, and distant relatives. The fact that the regular army and the *Landwehr* were on some distant battlefield constituted the greatest cause for concern in Scheiermacher's mind. The presence of relatives in the army should make Prussians more concerned about the victory of Germany over France instead of creating a desire for a short

[32] Hayes, *Essays on Nationalism,* p. 26.
[33] Schleiermacher, *Selected Sermons,* p. 77.
[34] *Ibid.,* p. 78.

campaign and a less-than-honorable peace. He felt that the more love the citizens had for those in the army and the reserves, the more they would love the mission on which the army was sent. The request that these loved ones should cease their holy work would be equal to disowning them. Instead of asking that the armies disband, the people of Prussia should encourage them to free all of Germany.[35]

Schleiermacher warned that the lot of the citizen who had to remain behind would in many ways be more difficult than that of the soldier engaged in battle. "Much precious blood will flow," he said, "many a beloved head will fall; let us not embitter their glorious lot by mournful fears and weak sorrow."[36] If the soldier must die for Germany, Germany must not be allowed to forget the sacrifice. Those on the home front would have to accept the responsibility for inscribing the greatest hour of Prussia in the annals of men's hearts, so that "this eternally memorable time may indeed be remembered, and that each descendant whom it concerns may say with just pride, 'There fought or there fell a relation of mine'."[37]

Schleiermacher concluded this nationalistic sermon with a fervent prayer in which he said:

Protect the beloved head of our king, and all the princes of his house, who are now with the army. Grant vision and strength to the commanders, courage to the soldiers, faithful steadfastness to all. And grant also, as Thou canst change and turn the fortune of war, that its blessing may not be lost to us; that each one may be purified and grow in the inner man; that we may grow stronger in confidence in Thee, and in obedience to Thy will, and obedience reaching even to death, like the obedience of Thy Son. Amen.[38]

The closing reference to the King in this sermon brings up an interesting point concerning Schleiermacher's nationalism. In 1813 he never seriously proposed to alter the role of the sovereign as the traditional leader of Prussia. The reforms which he advocated between 1808 and 1813 had been reforms which the King himself was to initiate. If followed to their logical conclusions these changes would have led to a rejuvination of monarchical conservatism.[39] The respect for German antiquity which Schleiermacher had acquired while he was with the romanticists was too deeply ingrained in him for him to withdraw his loyalty from the very

35 *Ibid.*, pp. 78–79.
36 *Ibid.*, p. 79.
37 *Ibid.*, p. 79.
38 *Ibid.*, p. 82.
39 Krieger, *The German Idea of Freedom*, pp. 177–178.

personification of Prussia's past. Friedrich Schlegel's interest in old German literature in which the central theme was the history of German royalty had been so effectively transmitted to Schleiermacher that he never doubted the propriety of the principles undergirding it.[40] The former romanticist's first doubts concerning the role of the kingship in the future German nation arose when he was forced to expand his interpretation of patriotism to fit all of Germany. Logically Germany could have a king as easily as Prussia but not on the basis of divine-right rule. A unified German nation would encompass many areas which were ruled in 1813 by monarchs claiming that they ruled by the will of God. Since Schleiermacher had already decided that only a unified Germany would merit the approval of the Lord, he was confronted with an obvious contradiction. Some principle besides the rule of a monarch by divine right would have to be utilized in selecting a sovereign for the German nation. Although he did not solve this problem during the War of Liberation, he did set forth some guiding principles concerning the part played by tradition in the selection of a king in a sermon on Trinity Sunday in 1813.

In this sermon, which was entitled "Necessity of the New Birth," Schleiermacher denied the validity of the doctrine of rule by divine right. He bluntly declared that the kingdom of the earthly prince did not extend "over every place where people act outwardly according to his will, but only where his will is also the real and common will of those who serve him and live under his rule."[41] If he had rephrased this statement he probably would have said that the will of the people in a nation like Prussia could be seen only in the collective traditions of the people. Friedrich Wilhelm was king of Prussia because the traditions of Prussia called for a Hohenzollern to rule the country, not because of divine right. Did this mean that his own allegiance to the king was diminished because the king did not occupy his throne by divine right? Quite the contrary! If it was the will of the people that the king lead the country, then it was certainly the will of the people as expressed in Prussia's traditions that the people follow the leadership of their king. Since these same traditions were present in all of Germany, unification would create no serious problems as far as the selection of a leader was concerned.[42]

The Trinity Church pastor was not the kind of nationalist who was

[40] Carlton J. H. Hayes, *The Historical Evolution of Modern Nationalism*, pp. 102–103.

[41] Schleiermacher, *Selected Sermons*, p. 102.

[42] Schleiermacher gave a great deal of attention to the theory of rule by divine right in his lectures on the theory of the state from 1817 until 1830. This will be discussed in Chapter 7.

capable only of telling others what the nation expected of them. He was careful to point out the fact that he was well aware of his own duties in helping to create a national German state. He felt that he was in no way excused from service to the state because he was a minister. His interpretation of his religious duties, which he equated with his national responsibilities, shows how clearly Schleiermacher resembled Carlton J. H. Hayes's definition of a nationalist as one who believes that he "owes his first and last duty to his nationality, that nationality is the ideal unit of political organization as well as the actual embodiment of cultural distinction, and that in the final analysis all other human loyalties must be subordinate to loyalty to the national state, that is, to national patriotism."[43] In a letter to a close friend, written in the summer of 1813, Schleiermacher described in precise terms the manner in which the minister must serve the national cause. He maintained that in time of war even the preacher of peace must take up the sword. While the soldiers send barrages of bullets toward the enemy the minister has to hurl a volley of words. The servant of God has no other choice. According to Schleiermacher a minister had not right to call men from the spiritual bondage of sin while he tolerated a condition where his people lived in bondage to a foreign power. To serve God, one must serve the state. The Trinity Church pastor did not actually assert that to be a Christian one must be a nationalist, but this was certainly implied when he confessed in a closing word in his letter, "I look upon it as an essential condition for the development of a people to be a truly Christian state, that its peculiar nationality should be relieved from the pressure of foreign dominations."[44] He could have made no stronger statement as a minister of the Gospel than to say that the test of a man's salvation in the sight of God depended upon that man's willingness to fight for his nationality.

Schleiermacher was well aware of the unique position which he occupied as a minister of the Church. The Protestant minister in Germany had always exercised a tremendous influence upon German society during a time of severe crisis, even more so than in other predominately Protestant countries. Schleiermacher added to his stature as a minister by consciously preaching sermons designed not only to lift the spirit of the listener but also to instill in that same listener a specific political point of

[43] Hayes, *Essays on Nationalism*, p. 26.
[44] Schleiermacher to Karl von Raumer, no place, no date, Friedrich Schleiermacher, *The Life of Friedrich Schleiermacher as Unfolded in His Autobiography and Letters*, II, 202.

view.[45] Because he consciously strived to bring about a specific, politically orientated response, he was greatly pleased when as a direct result of his nationalistic sermons to the students of Berlin the youth of the University requested sermons from him before they left for the battlefront. Since he never wrote them down after they were delivered, and in the confusion could rely upon no one to transcribe them, hardly any of these sermons are extant. Recollections and memoirs of those who heard the sermons furnish the only reliable record of what he said when he faced the same youth he had persuaded to go to war for the sake of Germany.

Schleiermacher's ability to inspire and console these young national soldiers is demonstrated in one of his sermons to a group of volunteers from the University of Berlin and the *gymnasium* just before they marched to Breslau in the spring of 1813. Their guns were stacked against the walls of Trinity Church as the uniformed young soldiers gathered to receive the sacraments from the frail preacher they had learned to admire. When Schleiermacher looked down from the Holy Desk upon these young men, who were joined in this final service by their friends and loved ones, he was not looking at strangers. These were students whom he knew by name. Here were people with whom he was intimately acquainted, but even when the impact of battle drove this close to his heart he saw before him the nucleus of a nation. He readily admitted to these devoted and idealistic young men that they were not responsible for the condition which they were being called upon to remedy. Prussia had stumbled into her depravity through her own willful choices while adhering to narrow concepts, proud aristocracy, and dead bureaucracy. Now they would have to pay for the sins of Prussia with their lives. With deep emotion he reminded this youthful audience that they had been aware of Prussia's pitiful record when they had willingly enlisted. In Schleiermacher's opinion this knowledge made their sacrifices even more sacred. Their task on the battlefields would not be easy, but it would be glorious. To emphasize the fact that in a nation-in-arms state all must share in the suffering as well as the rejoicing. Schleiermacher turned to the mothers of the recruits and with moving compassion concluded his sermon by saying, "Blessed is the womb that has borne such a son, blessed the breast that has nourished such a babe." A wave of emotion swept the congregation as Schleiermacher, with a burden in his heart that matched the weeping of the mothers and sons, pronounced what for many was a final Amen.[46]

[45] Richard Wittram, *Das Nationale als europäisches Problem*, p. 119.
[46] Schleiermacher, *Autobiography and Letters*, II, 202–204.

Schleiermacher almost lost his perspective because of his emotional involvement in preaching to the recruits from the University of Berlin. The usual anxieties of wartime were accentuated by the rumors, gossip, and fears that he encountered in his special work. He knew that courage would not compensate for Russian hesitancy and Austrian indecisiveness. When the poor communications brought news, the information was generally disheartening. Even a stout nationalist like Schleiermacher was physically shaken by the report that the battle of Grossgörschen had been lost on May 2 and 3, in spite of the superior position and the brave determination of the German youth in the ranks. He had even more reason to be disturbed by the news that Napoleon was east of the Elbe in Upper Lusatia, ready to launch an attack upon the allied armies or even to fall upon Berlin, which lay undefended to the north. No one could be sure where the next attack would take place and even staunch patriots like Friedrich Schleiermacher wavered between panic and courage in the face of danger.

In a letter to his wife, whom he had sent to Silesia for safety, Schleiermacher revealed the state of confusion he was experiencing with regard to the War. This letter, which was written in the very shadow of impending doom, demonstrated the faith which he had acquired as a nationalist. He expressed doubts about Prussia's allies, the armies, the military techniques being employed, and the resources, but not once did he indicate that he doubted that Germany would ultimately be victorious. He had looked upon the retreats of 1806 as the sign of cowardice in the ranks, for which there was no excuse. Now he told his wife that retreat by the allied armies would not constitute a victory for Napoleon. It would only mean that if Napoleonic armies pursued the retreating forces, they would find themselves in a land overflowing "not with milk and honey, but overflowing with the *Landsturm*."[47] Everything which once had brought a feeling of dismay to the Trinity preacher now was interpreted by him in an optimistic light. If he felt downhearted that the city of Berlin appeared to face imminent danger, he could take pleasure from the fact that the King had given orders for the *Landsturm* to defend the city. In the midst of the uncertainty surrounding the activities of the allied armies he saw the tangible determination of the people of Berlin as they built fortifications and dug entrenchments about the city. Even the women of the city volunteered to protect the symbol of their homeland. Schleiermacher had no way of knowing what the future held

[47] Schleiermacher to Henrietta Schleiermacher from Berlin, May 14, 1813, Reimer (ed.), *Aus Schleiermachers Leben,* II, 269.

for Germany but he promised his wife that under no circumstances could
the people of Germany expect Prussia to let them down as in 1806.[48]

Six days after Schleiermacher wrote this letter to his wife Napoleon
ended speculation concerning his intentions by attacking the allied armies
at Bautzen. Schleiermacher's contention that there had been a change in
the military spirit was borne out on the field of battle where the determination of the Prussian volunteers matched the fanaticism of the French
troops under the Republic. Napoleon won the battle, although he suffered severe casualties, but the Prussians won the moral victory which
they so desperately needed. The results of battles such as this seemed to
confirm Schleiermacher's hopes for the birth of a new Germany wrought
by the sacrifices of men fighting for a national cause.

Schleiermacher left a good description of the life of a busy nationalist
in a city facing possible annihilation. His lectures, in which he encouraged the young men of Berlin to fight for the sake of Germany, were so
successful that he no longer held any classes. In the place of the routine
of the classroom he substituted an exhausting schedule of continuous
effort. He devoted his morning hours to work on a committee for the
defense of the city. The afternoons, which once had been his time of
leisure were spent drilling with the *Landsturm*.[49] His evenings, supposedly set aside for meetings with the Church presbyterium, were taken
up with consecration sermons by the request of the King. The Trinity
pastor could honestly say that he was doing all that was humanly possible to increase the efficiency of the home front; yet even with all these
activities he was dissatisfied with his services for the war effort. He felt
a compassion for the people who longed for news but received none,
wanting to console these people in some way. He knew that there were
limits to a person's ability to pray for an army which he was not sure
even existed. In grasping for some element of hope to give to these people
he returned again and again to one simple truth in which the citizens of
Berlin would have to find comfort: the King remained in Berlin and
would fight to his death for his people.[50] If only the rest of Germany
could see the sacrifices of the Prussian people for them, Schleiermacher
was convinced that they would see the personification of the true German spirit.

He demonstrated his sense of patriotism toward his country in a heart-
touching way on May 15, 1813, when news arrived in Berlin that Napo-

[48] *Ibid.*, II, 269–270.
[49] *Ibid.*
[50] *Ibid.*

leon had just crossed the Elbe River, which meant that the fortifications around Berlin could not be completed in time to be effective. To facilitate the evacuation of the city the *Landsturm* had been called into service and, of course, this meant that Schleiermacher had to drop all his other activities and help with the evacuation. When the order for mobilization of the *Landsturm* was issued he had just had a reoccurrence of a severe stomach disorder, from which he had suffered for years, and was thus virtually incapacitated. The normal reaction of most people in this situation would have been to seek to be excused from *Landsturm* duties. Schleiermacher's only response to the summons to arms was to bemoan the fact that he had no ammunition on hand and could not secure any on Sunday. When the orders for the *Landsturm* were changed a few hours later he vowed, "I shall not fail to secure some ammunition tomorrow, so that I should not be exposed to public shame."[51]

The foregoing episodes from his life constitute a valid basis for three generalizations about Schleiermacher's nationalism in May, 1813. First, he felt that the only consideration open to a citizen was the welfare of the state, with health, safety, family, and occupation being matters of secondary importance. Second, he believed that the only way to help Germany achieve a free, unified nation was through the leadership of Prussia. Third, and most important, he had a tendency to oversimplify the problems standing in the way of German unification. He expected far too much too quickly.

An indication of the strength of his nationalism was his ability to adjust his views to fit realities. While he awaited the final orders for the evacuation of Berlin he grasped the unimportance of the city of Berlin. He admitted, though only to himself and his wife, that the decisions which would ultimately unite Germany would have to be made in Vienna. Call it realism or pessimism, he recognized that if Russia and Austria did not wish to see the German states unified under Prussia's leadership, Prussia would not be able to overcome their opposition. The attitude of these two countries' leaders convinced Schleiermacher that neither Austria nor Russia had any intention of allowing the dreams of German nationalism to become a reality.[52]

In spite of the premonition he had that Austria and Russia were the masters of Germany's destiny Schleiermacher did not abandon his hope that all Germans would be brought into a unified nation. Likewise, he

[51] *Ibid.*
[52] Schleiermacher to Henrietta Schleiermacher from Berlin, May 18, and May 22, 1813, Reimer (ed.), *Aus Schleiermachers Leben*, II, 273–275, and 277–278.

worked as diligently as ever on the entrenchments and in the *Landsturm*
maneuvers. The main difference in his attitude before and after the
Berlin crisis was that before the crisis he had believed that Prussia held
the key to German unification, whereas afterward he knew that other
countries were also to play a major role. Martin Buber's definition of
nationalism could well have been applied to the University of Berlin
theologian just before he acknowledged Austria's importance for German unification. In discussing the relationship between the terms "people," "nationality," and "nationalism," Buber said, "Being a people is
simply having eyes . . . which are capable of seeing." Nationality is more
like "having learned to perceive their function and to understand their
purpose; nationalism is like having diseased eyes and hence being constantly preoccupied with the fact of having eyes. A people is a phenomenon of life, nationality . . . is one of consciousness, nationalism one of
superconsciousness."[53]

The crisis over the defense of Berlin brought out another interesting
development in Schleiermacher's nationalism. He now expressed his
first feelings of anti-Semitism. He had never voiced any criticism of
Jewish theology, traditions, or culture before 1813, and perhaps would
not have done so then if he had not been under the kind of pressure that
brings out both the best and the worst in a man. The immediate cause for
his anti-Jewish outburst was the lack of Jewish cooperation with the
Landsturm. A few officials had fled the city when the French got close
enough to become a direct threat, but most of the officials and citizens
chose to obey the *Landsturm* law and fulfill their obligations. Schleiermacher had a chance to leave when the government rearranged the
work of the Ministry of the Interior, for most of the officials had been
given the choice of leaving or remaining to help defend Berlin. He wrote
his wife that he could understand how some could leave Berlin to accept
new responsibilities elsewhere. He could also have sympathy for the very
old and the very important who could serve no practical good by remaining in the city. However, he could muster nothing but contempt
for those who left Berlin for the sole purpose of avoiding their obligations and the group he singled out as having been most guilty of this
were the Jews. He confessed that he had within himself the most un-
Christian feeling toward these traitors, for he hoped that "the downright
cowards, either from among the court servants or from among the citizenry will get their just retribution, for a great many people, and es-

[53] Salo W. Baron, *Modern Nationalism and Religion*, p. 3.

pecially a great many rich Jews, are said to have fled."[54] He saw no
room in Prussia for any group, be it linguistic, religious, or ethnic, which
would put its own safety above the good of the nation, nor could he fore-
see a place for them in a unified Germany.

If one were seeking for one single piece of evidence that would indicate that Schleiermacher's nationalistic viewpoint had become more
realistic by May, 1813, than it had been until that time, that single event
was the visit which Ernst Moritz Arndt paid to him. It is necessary to
understand the relationship between Arndt and Schleiermacher before
1813 to understand clearly what this visit meant. Schleiermacher had
met Arndt in 1809 when Arndt fled from Rügen to Berlin to avoid prosecution for anti-French agitation. Arndt took refuge in the home of Georg
Andreas Reimer, the owner of the Realschulbuchhandlung in Berlin and
an intimate friend of Friedrich Schleiermacher for a number of years.[55]
Because of Reimer's contacts Arndt was initiated into the Charlottenburger Bund, which was one of the many patriotic clubs in Berlin.
Gneisenau, Reil, Schele, Gruner, and Boyen, who were members of the
Bund, immediately recognized in Arndt the same spirit which motivated
them to risk their lives for the sake of nationalism.[56] Arndt's reputation
was further enhanced through the Reading Society [Lesende Gesell-
schaft], which was a patriotic club that met in Reimer's home. This is
where Arndt and Schleiermacher became acquainted, since Schleiermacher attended the irregularly held meetings of the society.[57] Both men
immediately recognized a common ground between them. Arndt's *Spirit
of the Times,* which he had written shortly before meeting Schleiermacher, bore a remarkable resemblance to the Trinity Church pastor's
sermon "A Nation's Duty in a Time of War," which has been extensively
quoted in this chapter. Both men were extremely idealistic about German nationalism, a fact which led them to jump to the same superficial
conclusions concerning the possibility of a national German state.[58]

Arndt lived with Reimer until the spring of 1810, a full year before
Schleiermacher came to realize that all hope for Germany lay in a national awakening led by Prussia for the sake of all of Germany. After
two years in Swedish Pomerania, Arndt returned to Berlin shortly before

[54] Schleiermacher to Henrietta Schleiermacher from Berlin, May, 1813, Reimer
(ed.), *Aus Schleiermachers Leben,* II, 281–282.
[55] Alfred G. Pundt, *Arndt and the National Awakening in Germany,* p. 71.
[56] *Ibid.*; Müsebeck, *Ernst Moritz Arndt: Ein Lebensbild,* I, 266.
[57] Pundt, *Arndt and the National Awakening,* p. 87.
[58] Wittram, *Das Nationale als europäisches Problem,* pp. 119–123.

traveling to Russia to join the exiled Stein.[59] In January, 1813, Stein
and Arndt left Moscow for Königsberg, where Stein had permission to
call the provincial diet of East Prussia and start an uprising in Germany.
By May, Arndt was working for Stein in the city of Dresden, only to be
forced out when the French threat caused the evacuation of the city.
Stein then sent Arndt to Berlin with the intention of having him determine Sweden's attitude toward a military alliance with the Allied Powers
against France.[60] This was the mission on which Arndt was working
when he visited Schleiermacher in Berlin on May 28, 1813, in the company of Johann Eichhorn, Savigny, and Schele. Arndt wanted Schleiermacher to go to military headquarters on a mission apparently connected with his own trip to Stralsund.

Schleiermacher's decision not to undertake the assignment was one
of the most revealing of his life. It certainly was not a case of snap judgment on his part for he had a number of good reasons for not taking the
trip. His health was a factor in his decision not to participate in the mission, for he had endured a great deal of strain from 1806 until 1813,
and the spells of stomach trouble were becoming more regular. There
was also the matter of his family, for Schleiermacher had become more
and more conscious of his family responsibilities in the year 1813. However, neither of these would have prevented him from going to Königsberg if he had really felt that he could do some good for the cause of
German unification, for he himself had said on a number of occasions
that health and family considerations were of secondary importance to
the nationalist. He did not wish to serve with Arndt because he no longer
believed that the activities in which Arndt and Stein were involved offered the correct solution for Germany's problems.[61] Germany had not
followed the lead of Prussia in rising against the French. Instead, the
German areas occupied by French troops either sat complacently by and
let the issue be decided elsewhere, or acted on behalf of France against
Prussia. To Schleiermacher this meant that the German people were
not yet ready to become a nation. Stein and Arndt did not represent the
spirit of all of Germany. They only represented the desires of Russia
and Austria to drive Napoleon from Germany. Neither of these powers
wished to see the national movement which had started in Prussia spread
to other areas of Germany. By assisting Russia and Austria against French

---

[59] Pundt, *Ardnt and the National Awakening*, pp. 88–90.

[60] Ernst M. Arndt, *Ernst Moritz Arndts sämmtliche Werke*, II, 126–129.

[61] Schleiermacher to Henrietta Schleiermacher from Berlin, May 28, 1813,
Reimer (ed.), *Aus Schleiermachers Leben*, II, 284–285.

forces, Schleiermacher would only be perpetuating the very system he had learned to detest. Since he would have been wasting his time trying to convince Arndt that this was the case, he did the next best thing. He excused himself from the proposed mission.

Schleiermacher reiterated his pessimism about a nationalistic war a short time later in a letter to his wife. He had sent her to Silesia for her own safety, only to learn that the French had advanced into the same area. When he wrote to assure her that things would somehow turn out for the best he could not help crying out in despair, "Everything around me looks pathetically gloomy, and I am on the verge of giving up the whole cause." He went on to say that perhaps he had been mistaken about the national awakening. Maybe what he had seen in the faces of the volunteers as they prepared for battle only two months before had been an illusion for both himself and the young men. Germany was not yet ready to be a mature nation of people with a common purpose. The questions he asked himself indicated that the reverses and the retreats had covered him with the same blanket of dismay as had been spread over the population. If only Austria would make a move, thought Schleiermacher. Why must Sweden hold out for a higher price? Why must Russia and Prussia deal with Sweden as though they were casually shopping at a market? "And what about the population?" asked Schleiermacher. "Good God, can we count on them? How many are there who really are moved by patriotism? . . . Oh, God, my beloved. There is nothing left for a person to look forward to under these conditions except a fitting death."[62] Beyond a doubt this was the darkest moment and most helpless hour in his life. He had reached the state of mind where he could do nothing for his family or his nationality except pray for both and devote to each a passive love.[63]

In the light of this despondency it was not surprising that he took on an air of indifference toward the events of international diplomacy which transpired after the beginning of June, 1813. Trusting in Russia and Austria had proved to be a futile pastime. All of the talk about the Czar's liberalism only created grave doubts in his mind. When an armistice was agreed upon by the contending forces in June, the despondent nationalist should have remonstrated loudly against it as a sign of poor faith toward Prussia by the allies. Instead of crying out against the armistice as he

[62] Schleiermacher to Henrietta Schleiermacher from Berlin, May 31, 1813, *ibid.*, II, 288–289.

[63] Schliermacher to Henrietta Schleiermacher from Berlin, June 2, 1813, *ibid.*, II, 290.

would have done six months earlier he welcomed it as a chance to be reunited with his wife. His former demand for a spirit of sacrifice became a mere whisper when he wrote to his wife, "I am beside myself with joy when I think about it . . . Never again, dearest Jette, will we be separated again like this." He went on to tell her that, regardless of the peril of the nation, he was not going to put it ahead of her welfare.[64]

His expectations for a national war of liberation and for help from Russia and Austria against France took a strange twist when his dreams materialized, for he discovered that he no longer valued what he once had sought. He had hoped for the growth and development of Prussian patriotism. When Prussia regained its military courage, he decided that this was not enough. The real goal for him was German nationalism. The only way to achieve this much desired German freedom would be to force France from German soil. By June, 1813, when the defeat of France was a distinct possibility he had decided that even a victory over France would not breathe into the hearts of the German people the necessary desire for national independence. He summarized his feelings on the lack of a nationalistic zeal in Germany in a letter to Friedrich Schlegel in June, 1813, in which he wrote that he could not believe that Germany could ever be satisfied merely with victory over France. He did not know how long it would take for the Germans to rise above the petty differences and difficulties of 1813, but the wars with France must surely produce something besides empty sacrifices. Almost prophetically, he was pointing to the reaction which would soon sweep Prussia and all of Germany, undoing all that the bloody battles had accomplished in uniting Germans.[65]

Schleiermacher's disgust over what he considered a temporarily lost cause explains his lack of direct patriotic activity after June, 1813. Even though the war with France was to last for almost another year he ceased to lift his voice to arouse the people. His sense of nationalism was too strong to allow him to perpetuate or stimulate a set of circumstances which would run counter to the best interests of Germany. In fact, he turned his whole attention toward activities that soon placed him in opposition to the government of Prussia. Georg Reimer had edited the *Correspondent,* a semipolitical journal in Berlin, until he felt that his other duties would force him to give up the job. When Reimer resigned

[64] Schleiermacher to Henrietta Schleiermacher from Berlin, June 8, 1813, *ibid.,* II, 294.

[65] Schleiermacher to Friedrich Schlegel from Berlin, June 12, 1813, Meisner (ed.), *Schleiermacher als Mensch,* II, 189.

the position he persuaded Schleiermacher to assume the editorship though Friedrich had a great many misgivings about the work before he even started. As he told his wife, "It will place a great deal of strain upon me, I know. I will have to do things to which I am not accustomed and about which I know very little, and there will be quarrels with the government and the silly censorship."[66] Thus he anticipated trouble with the government before he began working on the *Correspondent*.

His services as editor of this journal during the War of Liberation constituted the last effort on his part to mold the nationalistic thinking of the people of Berlin before the period of reaction set in. The difficulties which he had anticipated materialized when through his comments in the *Correspondent* he became involved in a verbal war between the critics and the defenders of Stein. Scharnhorst's death after the battle of Grossgörschen led E. M. Arndt to write a song in his memory entitled *Auf Scharnhorsts Tod*. His death also called forth a vehement debate on the circumstances surrounding Stein's dismissal in December, 1808.[67] These memories, which in themselves would have been enough to bring to Schleiermacher's mind the bitterness of 1809, were augmented by fresh incidents which aroused him as much as the previous crime against Stein. The King dismissed the *Landsturm,* which had been a shining example of what the new Germany should be like. This decision by the King coincided with a very unpopular reprimand given to an army officer by the government. All these acts signified to the *Correspondent* editor a complete reversal of the few progressive tendencies which the Prussians had demonstrated. He felt that he had no alternative but to denounce the *Landsturm* decision and the reprimand incident as a continuation of the old conspiracy against Stein and the spirit of reform. When he took his firm stand he became the object of a subtle persecution. The government refused to send him official notices for publication, which was its way of pretending that he and his journal did not even exist. Old friends, who had once respected him for his patriotism, were intimidated by Prussian officials and as a result had to choose between their friendship for him and their relationship with the government.

Schleiermacher endured the pressure upon his family and friends as long as he could and then finally, on July 14, 1813, he openly attacked the government for its handling of the war effort against the French. The primary object of his wrath was the participation by the Prussian

[66] Schleiermacher to Henrietta Schleiermacher from Berlin [June or July] 24, 1813, Reimer (ed.), *Aus Schleiermachers Leben*, II, 300–301.

[67] Pundt, *Arndt and the National Awakening*, p. 111.

government in the peace talks being carried on at that time between the
Allied Powers and France at Prague. Though his editorial was heavily
censored, one can still see Schleiermacher striking out as a vigorous nationalist at what he considered to be an abandonment of the chances for
German unification. The signs of a loss of determination to carry on the
war against France were too unmistakable. If the war was to be resumed after the armistice was over, the loss of nationalist zeal would
prevent the furtherance of nationalistic hopes for Germany. If it was
not resumed Germany would remain precisely as she existed when the
armistice began. The promises, the hopes, the dreams, the rights, and
the heritage of Germany had been betrayed by the greedy negotiators
who controlled the destiny of the German people.[68]

When Friedrich Wilhelm learned of the attack upon the integrity of
the government by the editor of the *Correspondent*, he immediately
issued a cabinet order, dated July 17, in which he stated that he had
taken all that he intended to take from Schleiermacher. The King admitted that part of the blame for the inflammatory editorial must go to
the censor, who had been careless in his work, but, said Friedrich Wilhelm, "This does not lessen the guilt of Schleiermacher, who on various
occasions has already shown tendencies which I absolutely will not tolerate."[69] By the cabinet order Schleiermacher was dismissed from his
duties with the *Correspondent* and told to leave Berlin within forty-eight
hours. However, as was the case with so many such acts by the King,
the terms of the order were eased considerably and Schleiermacher was
merely reprimanded for his public indiscretions. Having taken pride in
himself when he discovered that he possessed a degree of toughness of
which he had not been aware, Schleiermacher tried in a letter to Georg
Reimer to brush aside the entire turn of events by saying that "the good
cause will somehow prove to be victorious. My difficulties have really
served only to amuse me, since the whole affair is too absurd to cause a
real annoyance."[70]

He may have felt that the attitude of the Prussian government was a
minor problem in his life, but the Prussian government was not prone
to dismiss lightly what it considered unfavorable conduct. Schuckmann,
Schleiermacher's superior in the Ministry of the Interior, was sent by
the chancellor to warn him that he faced dismissal from all his official

[68] Klein, *Die Befreiung*, pp. 225–227.
[69] *Ibid.*, p. 227.
[70] Schleiermacher to Georg Reimer from Berlin, July 24, 1813, Reimer (ed.),
Aus Schleiermachers Leben, II, 305–306.

responsibilities if he did not stop criticizing the government in the *Correspondent*. Such action would have terminated his pastorship of the Trinity Church, and his professorship at the University of Berlin, as well as his editorship. Schuckmann informed him that his opposition to official policies amounted to treason and that if he continued to anger the King he would be considered a traitor to the state. He concluded the reprimand with assurances to Schleiermacher that he considered him to be an upright and sincere man and that he was extremely sorry he had been selected to deliver such an unpleasant message from the government.[71]

Schleiermacher did not need a messenger to tell him that his nationalism was no longer acceptable to the King. He had sensed that for a good while. He must have been well aware that unless he changed his thinking about the future of Germany he would continue to be a thorn in the flesh of the government. The reprimand which he had received through Schuckmann had been only a polite advance notice of what he could expect if he disobeyed his instructions. Thus his life as a patriotic preacher trying to usher into Germany a new age of national consciousness came to an end. From that time on he had to find new means of expressing his ideas without the protection of government affiliation. The tragedy of Schleiermacher's life as a nationalist is that he spent half of his life preparing for a series of events which were at best only an illusion, and the other half of his life looking back upon them.

[71] *Ibid.*, II, 306–307.

|||||||| 6. SCHLEIERMACHER DURING THE PERIOD OF REACTION

As Boyd Shafer pointed out in *Nationalism: Myth and Reality,* nationalism is irrational.[1] The man who claims that nationality is the sole foundation upon which to build a state usually does so on the basis of personal feelings, vague influences, excessive pride, or any one of a multitude of intangible emotions that go into the make-up of a nationalist. Seldom does the nationalist arrive at his point of view on the basis of concrete historical research. He is likewise oblivious to facts or contemporary trends which may contradict or nullify his nationalistic opinions, and since he seldom considers such factors as public safety, personal safety, or official disfavor while he is spreading his nationalistic propaganda, he is somewhat of an ivory-tower idealist. His nationalistic dreams are thus usually quite far removed from reality. However, the weakness of nationalism—a lack of rational identification with historical facts—is also its chief strength, for the nationalist is not subject to the day-to-day encouragements and discouragements which affect the political viewpoints of the average person. He has a nationalistic messianic hope that rises above, and even conquers, the defeats which would completely demoralize those who are more logical and rational in their approach to political problems.

In the light of these unusual characteristics of the nationalist a valid test of the sincerity of his devotion to his nationality would be his determination to continue working for nationalistic goals when all evidence indicates that he is wrong and that there is no possible way for his longed-for national state to exist. If the nationalist can continue to hope for the seemingly impossible and to reach for the unobtainable, then his nationalism obviously is part of his character and not just a passing fancy. Friedrich Schleiermacher's nationalism had to undergo nearly two decades of testing after 1813. Throughout the entire period of the political

[1] Boyd Shafer, *Nationalism: Myth and Reality,* pp. 5–11, 47–56.

reaction (the name given generally to the period of conservatism in Europe after the defeat of Napoleon) he encountered one frustration after another in his nationalistic effort. Knowing that he would never live to see the unification of Germany and all that unification would bring in the way of cultural achievements and political strength, he nevertheless continued to preach and teach the ideals of German nationalism. That he could do so in the face of the official opposition of the Prussian government and the obvious unconcern of the German people was a testimony to the depths of the devotion he felt to his nationality.

As has already been noted Schleiermacher could see in 1813 that Stein's reform program was doomed and that the Prussian government was already reverting to the conservative, narrow policies of the pre-Napoleonic period. He had not been able to see at that time, however, that this shift toward conservatism would make his theories on nationalism extremely unpopular in official Prussian circles. His fiery sermons in 1813 had been useful in stimulating the popular sentiment of the Prussian people for the War of Liberation but the popular support for the war effort had been only a temporary expedient for destroying the power of the French army. As soon as victory over Napoleon became a certainty Austrian leaders, especially Metternich and Gentz, began to exert influence upon Friedrich Wilhelm to stop the nationalistic German spirit. Schleiermacher had foreseen the dominant part Austria would play in determining Prussia's future but he had had no concept of the thoroughness with which political questions would be handled from Vienna.[2] Because of the change in the attitude of Prussia's government toward further public demonstrations on behalf of German nationalism after 1813, he found that he was now almost an enemy of the state which he had served as a loyal teacher and preacher before the reaction. By late 1814 he came to know the full measure of official disfavor to the same degree and extent that he had once known official favor. Instead of harboring recriminations toward the Prussian government because of the alteration of his relationship to the state he exercised a marvelous patience, believing all the while that some day the work he and others had begun in 1813 toward building a national German state would come

[2] Golo Mann, *Secretary of Europe: The Life of Friedrich Gentz, Enemy of Napoleon*, pp. 207–231; Friedrich Meinecke, *Weltbürgertum und Nationalstaat: Studien zur Genesis des deutschen Nationalstaates*, pp. 206–222; Alfred Stern, *Geschichte Europas seit den Verträgen von 1815 bis zum Frankfurter Frieden von 1871*, I, 279–345, 380–480.

to fruition. Until that hour arrived he was determined that he would prepare as much of the groundwork necessary for German unification as the Prussian government would tolerate.

The extent of Schleiermacher's disappointment over the course of German nationalism during the War of Liberation was revealed in his negative attitude toward Allied successes over the French forces in the spring of 1814. Even though he had spent seven years trying to create a determination in Prussia to fight France, the joy that should have come from Allied victories was missing. He knew in late 1813 and early 1814 that Prussia had already lost all hope for German unification. This could only mean that the battles being fought by brave Prussians, who thought they were fighting for a new era in Germany, were needless sacrifices. These victories would only hurry Prussia's return to the dead aristocracy of the eighteenth century and he saw no reason for celebrating a return to the past.

The first instance where he expressed his belief that German nationalism was quickly becoming a lost cause during the War of Liberation was a letter which he wrote to Charlotte von Kathen in the spring of 1814, at the climax of the War. In this letter he admitted that he did not share in the enthusiasm sweeping Prussia because he could see the full price Germany would have to pay for Prussian blunders. He expressed the opinion that Germany would have been better off in the long run if Prussia had been defeated. The hopes that he had nurtured for Prussia as a leader in German unification were wholly dependent upon a condition which would literally force the rest of Germany to recognize the need to follow Prussian leadership. But if Prussia acted as though she were a mere pawn in the hands of the major powers or a power-hungry state setting out to annex vast stretches of territory, her ability to lead the other states of Germany would be destroyed.[3]

He conceded that tremendous changes had been made in Prussia since the national awakening had dawned upon the land the year before, but even the fact that some alterations had been made during the War of Liberation caused him to feel downhearted. He felt that the changes which had been made by the government had been forced upon the administration in the face of national extinction. In other words, the King had led the administration to make reforms out of fear and not out of a feeling of duty to the German people. To make matters worse, Schleiermacher complained, only about half of the needed reforms had

[3] Schleiermacher to Charlotte von Kathen from Berlin, April 4, 1814, Georg Reimer (ed.), *Aus Schleiermachers Leben in Briefen,* II, 309–310.

been brought about. He dejectedly noted that the government of Prussia
had been like the dying man who would promise anything to be allowed
to live. Once the danger was gone Prussia would suppress the temporarily handy expediency of nationalism, which had given life to the dying
state. The Berlin pastor had expected the War of Liberation to lift Prussia to a new level of national pride in German traditions. Instead he saw
Prussia about to descend to a new level of narrow provincialism. He
could not refrain from asking if Prussia had learned nothing from the
struggle except the baseness of the French and the treachery of the
Saxons.[4] While he may not have been sure that there was no chance for
an increase in national awareness at some future date, he wrote in the
conclusion to the letter that he was fairly certain that for the time being
the possibility of some immediate manifestation of German nationalism
in Prussia was out of the question.

In another letter written in the spring of 1814 he dealt with the problem of the future of the nationalist cause in Germany. Jacobi, the man
with whom Schleiermacher was corresponding, had written to him concerning a fine point in theology. Schleiermacher was attempting to
answer him in a carefully worded theological document that had no political overtones whatsoever. In spite of his concentration upon the question at hand the Trinity Church pastor revealed the extent to which the
problem of German unification occupied his thinking when he digressed
several times from his theological topic to touch upon the subject of
Germany's future. The key fact which he brought to Jacobi's attention
was that one can never turn back to an earlier stage of development once
history has passed over or superseded it. It was just as true for ecclesiastical as for political history that historical continuity always turned the
chaos of events into an understandable process. To try to go back to
eighteenth-century interpretations of the scriptures on the basis of outdated methods of biblical criticism would be disastrous for scholarly
theology. To go back to outmoded political concepts in the light of the
progress of the German people toward a sense of unity and interdepend-
ence would be even more ruinous.[5] Trying to return to a past era would
be like trying to return to a state of infancy. Progress in this sense of the
word was impossible to change or reverse. Of course, he was not advocating that historical determinism applied to German nationalism as
much as he was stating his convictions concerning the need for respect

[4] *Ibid.*, II, 310.
[5] Schleiermacher to Jacobi from Berlin [Spring, 1814], *ibid.*, II, 350–352.

for historical continuity.[6] After all, he maintained, Prussia had taken some definite steps toward leading Germany into a new era. Even if the tide of reaction turned Prussia from this path for the time being, eventually the historical continuity of these acts of national awakening would demand fulfillment. He knew that he might have to wait a number of years to see the end of the reaction. Perhaps he might not see it in his lifetime, but someday Germany would renew the efforts she had made in the spring of 1813 to form a German nation.

A third indicator of Schleiermacher's belief in the ultimate victory of nationalism and his lack of confidence in an immediate victory at the end of the Napoleonic wars was a sermon he preached in the Trinity Church in Berlin in 1814. His object in the sermon was to show that if aid is extended to one in need the person who accepts the help creates an eternal debt, which can never be truly repaid. The biblical narration around which he built his sermon was the story of the man on the road to Jerusalem who fell among thieves, losing all his possessions and being left for dead. In spite of the man's obvious need he was passed on two occasions by men who were able but unwilling to render aid. When help finally was offered to him it was by a lowly Samaritan, from whom no self-respecting Jew would have accepted assistance. According to Schleiermacher the injured man lost much to the robbers but he gained much more from the care extended to him out of a spirit of love. Once the Trinity Church pastor had retold the biblical account of the good Samaritan so graphically that no one could mistake the details of the narrative he carefully drew a parallel between what had happened to the destitute man and the precarious position of Prussia up to 1813. Prussia, like the wounded man, had been robbed and beaten at Tilsit, after which the countries that had been capable of helping her had turned their back upon her needs. As in the case of the good Samaritan, when help finally came to Prussia, it was from the least likely source—the common man motivated by a spirit of national love. Like the injured man on the road, Prussia had not stopped to question the devotion of the one who offered assistance. Instead she had even encouraged the sacrifices of the common people—an encouragement to which the masses had responded with undying credit to themselves. Here the similarities between the two stories broke down, for in the biblical account the man who had received the aid had acknowledged an eternal debt that he knew he could never repay without matching the love which had gone out to him. Instead of giving

[6] Richard Brandt, *The Philosophy of Schleiermacher*, pp. 134–136.

thanks for the aid that had been given, the Prussian government had acted as though it had deserved the sacrifices offered up on the battle-field.[7] Prussia recognized no debt; Prussia had no love. Someday she would come to realize the immensity of her obligation to the people of all of Germany, but until that time the people would have to consider nationalism as an unpaid debt of the government.

These documents from 1814 not only indicate that for the first time in his life Schleiermacher had to defend the tenets of nationalism; they also reveal the responsibility he felt. Many times between the years 1806 and 1814 he had preached sermons in order to stimulate patriotic devotion on the part of his Berlin congregation, sometimes at the risk of his position or his safety during the French occupation. During these years of service in the pulpit he espoused nationalism, feeling all the while that the government supported his views as noble and worthwhile. By 1814 the situation had changed so radically that what once had been encouraged by the government was now denied and suppressed. The alteration of the Prussian government's attitude toward nationalism tended to reduce to a bare minimum the ranks of those who had formerly led in the struggle against France. Since many of the participants in the War of Liberation were basically opposed to the national aspirations of patriots like Schleiermacher and since many of those who agreed with the nationalists were intimidated into silence by the government, the need grew daily for carefully argued declarations on the proper relationship between the state of Prussia and the rest of Germany. This tremendous responsibility for bolstering the weakening voice of German nationalism in Prussia was viewed by Schleiermacher as a personal duty which he could not ignore. His main problem was in selecting a means to continue speaking on behalf of nationalism with maximum effectiveness while incurring minimum risk. Sermons had always been an effective means of arousing the people but the long-range effectiveness of indoctrination from the pulpit was questionable because the pulpit messages were too irregular to be of real value. Sensing as he did that he could have little effect on the government's attitude with sermons he chose to use the pen instead of the pulpit when the time came for him to express his views. At the same time he did not court government displeasure by attacking issues concerning which no possible success could be achieved. He was no coward—a fact which he had demonstrated in Berlin in May, 1813, and September, 1808. He just could see no point in exposing himself to the

[7] Friedrich Schleiermacher, *Sämmtliche Werke, Predigten*, I, 392–394.

reactionary Prussian authorities unless something significant could result.

An outstanding example of Schleiermacher's scholarly approach to the problem of expressing his nationalistic views without placing himself in a difficult position was a paper which he presented to the Royal Academy in Berlin on March 24, 1814. In it he discussed the democratic, aristocratic, and monarchical forms of government as though he were comparing three philosophical points of view. He very cleverly developed the part that tradition must play in the form of government which a people select for their nation. Then he combined this idea of historical continuity with the principle of the organic structure of the state. The logical conclusion which one sees in the paper, though Schleiermacher never actually said it, was that Germany must have a government representing all the traditions of the many German states. Though not advocating the overthrow of the Prussian government in the strict sense of the word, he was saying that the governments of any of the particularist states actually had no right to exist and that some day they would be either voluntarily or forcibly replaced.

He pointed out that a form of government could not be imported or copied from another country because no two groups of people would have identical traditions. When the time came for the particularist states to form a government consisting of all the German territories the German people would be resourceful enough to construct a governmental system which would fit their own needs. The actual type of government was immaterial. The government would function smoothly as long as the administrators were well qualified, a fact which meant for Schleiermacher that they were aware of the traditions of the people.[8] He warned his fellow scholars at the Royal Academy that it would be the height of folly to try to devise on paper a perfect state system of government for Germany. Men had tried this for centuries and the only results of the efforts of these "state-builders" were confusion. The drafters of the master plans for society always ignored the fact that a person tended to design the type of government which was best suited for his own personal tastes and habits.[9] Given the freedom to do so the people of Germany would construct a constitutional government which would be a perfect reflection of German tastes and customs. The present Prussian government was an artificial creation which neither reflected nor resembled the true spirit of the citizenry—a condition which would never be altered as long as Prussia's people were denied the right to partici-

[8] Schleiermacher, *Sämmtliche Werke, Zur Philosophie,* II, 249.
[9] *Ibid.,* II, 250.

pate in their government. He thus argued for a national German state by showing that particularistic administrations like that of Prussia simply did not reflect the will of the German people.

The use of scholarly articles which dealt with rather abstract subjects allowed Schleiermacher a certain degree of freedom legally to criticize the Prussian government by pointing to nationalism as a suitable solution to Germany's problems without mentioning Prussia or openly attacking the administration of the state by Friedrich Wilhelm III. The Prussian government was, of course, not ignorant of these legal but still questionable activities, but the only noticeable official reaction was the maintenance of a close scrutiny of Schleiermacher's classes to see that he was not acquiring too large a following among the students and faculty at the University of Berlin. This was certainly a milder treatment than that meted out to vociferous nationalists like Arndt and Jahn.[10] In effect Schleiermacher and the Prussian government had reached a stalemate by late 1814. Having said enough to justify his dismissal from the University of Berlin, he temporarily refrained from making any antagonistic overtures. He was awaiting the outcome of the negotiations of the Congress of Vienna, which met in the fall of 1814 to restore order to the chaos which Napoleon had brought to Europe. As long as there was even a remote possibility that Friedrich Wilhelm could gain from the Vienna diplomats concessions which might possibly revitalize nationalistic tendencies in Germany, Schleiermacher felt obligated to say nothing that might in any way complicate the negotiations.

As the weeks slipped into months and the negotiations at Vienna produced nothing in the way of encouragement for the nationalist, he became convinced that nothing worth while would ever result from the death of so many German youths, who had died thinking that they were helping to create a new unified Germany. This failure of the Congress of Vienna to take progressive steps with regard to the promises made to the people of the various states by their governments during the War of Liberation confirmed his worst fears for the future of nationalism in Germany for many years to come. Ironically, Schleiermacher's self-imposed silence on nationalism was broken by the publication of a fairly obscure sermon[11] which he had preached in 1812 but which had not been printed until shortly before the end of the military campaigns of 1814. In this sermon he had likened the experiences of disappointed nationalists to the disappointments which Jesus had encountered in dealing with his disci-

[10] Ernst Müsebeck, *Ernst Moritz Arndt: Ein Lebensbild*, pp. 506–564.
[11] Schleiermacher, *Sämmtliche Werke, Predigten*, I, 449–461.

ples. The sermon, which had been aimed at a listless population in 1812, could very easily be interpreted as an attack upon the government in 1814 and 1815. Because of this weird trick of fate Friedrich appeared to take a strong stand against the Prussian government—the very thing he was trying to avoid.

In the main, throughout the sermon he stressed the theme that with Jesus suffering and failures usually resulted from the acts of unreliable people, just as they did with people involved in a national awakening. The concepts of Jesus taught fundamental truths to potential disciples. When the disciples tried to apply these principles to their own lives the element of human error had to be overcome. This did not mean that Jesus should have abandoned his mission among men or that he should have produced a more practical ethical system. It simply meant that Jesus had to be extremely patient and understanding in the light of man's imperfection. Schleiermacher certainly must have had nineteenth-century Germany in mind when he said with reference to Jesus that one must not base his plans upon people, for the weakness of man in a time of trial causes even the most carefully prepared plans to fail.[12] He had not hesitated in 1812 to declare his belief that Germany's unification was a sign of the manifestation of the will of God, but he almost played the part of the prophet when he said that the idea of unification would not become an actuality until the appearance of a dynamic personality who could overcome the weakness of German leadership. As Schleiermacher stated it, "My friends, let us learn this from the Savior. There is nothing more bitter than to learn that you have built your hopes and expectations, only to learn later that you invested your faith in vain."[13] When this sermon was delivered in 1812 his references to weakness and compromise had been aimed at the masses who were failing to respond to the challenge of a national awakening. Since by 1815 the people had already demonstrated their willingness to die for their homeland, his remarks no longer were appropriate. On the other hand, the reactionary elements of the Prussian government had so successfully squelched the popular enthusiasm in the spring of 1814 that Schleiermacher's remarks seemed to be aimed directly at them.

In 1812 Schleiermacher had said that he could sympathize with Jesus because he, like the Master, had preached a message to which the people had temporarily responded with enthusiasm. The superficiality of the popular response had seemed to him to be worse than no response at all.

[12] *Ibid.*, I, 449.
[13] *Ibid.*, I, 449–451.

This lack of wholehearted enthusiasms had caused him to remark that "we are too often turned toward despondency when we note that the movements of the people toward the right is only a passing, superficial phenomenon."[14] He made specific reference to the fickleness of the populace when he predicted that the leaders would become disgusted "with their praise, their sense of honor, their devotion, when we see on other occasions that they follow others who are thoroughly opposed."[15] This was the same as saying that Friedrich Wilhelm, Hardenberg, and Altenstein were in opposition to the will of the people of Prussia. Again Schleiermacher had said in 1812 in a patriotic way that which would appear in 1815 to be a denunciation of the Prussian government.

The most damaging part of the sermon for Schleiermacher was the section devoted to cowardice, where he said that the followers of Jesus had not been alarmed over the possibility of struggle, opposition, or sacrifice so long as these were intangibles. When these possibilities became realities the disciples abandoned Jesus to His lonely death. The disciples of the Savior had undergone the same experience as the military and political leaders of Prussia. They had the nerve to approach the prize of victory but not the fortitude to grasp it. Schleiermacher had wasted no words in describing how he felt about political or personal cowardice, saying, "I cannot begin to tell what thorough debasement there is in this condition; with what emotion, bordering on contempt, the noble and vigorous should look down upon it."[16] This charge of outright cowardice aimed at the Prussian people was easily interpreted to be a thrust at the King and his court. To make matters worse he invoked the judgment of God upon any who would dare allow the national movement to falter or fail, saying, "Where ruin creeps in, immediately behind it comes, as it did in the time of Christ, the judgment of God."[17]

Schleiermacher's invoking of the wrath of God upon the enemies of Prussia had pleased Prussian officialdom as long as France was that enemy, but by 1815 he was seemingly calling for that same judgment upon the heads of the very men who had once so ardently encouraged him to preach patriotic sermons. One can easily understand the embarrassment of the government over sermons like this, especially in the light of the unwillingness of Friedrich Wilhelm to keep the promises made to the Prussian people during the crucial years of 1813 and 1814.

[14] *Ibid.*, I, 453.
[15] *Ibid.*, I, 453–454.
[16] *Ibid.*, I, 457–458.
[17] *Ibid.*, I, 460–461.

The first tangible results of the strained relations between Schleiermacher and Chancellor Altenstein resulting from Schleiermacher's sermons and his nationalistic reputation was Schleiermacher's departure from the section on instruction under the Ministry of the Interior.[18] Occupying an official position and yet criticizing the policies of the King and the Chancellor as he did, he had naturally been a source of discomfort for the government. However, if he thought that his withdrawal from government service would allow him to live a life of quiet contemplation, he was seriously mistaken. He immediately became involved in three separate controversial issues which stemmed from his devotion to German nationalism and which required that he very carefully analyze his nationalistic aspirations. As a result of these self-evaluations he repeatedly found himself facing only two possible alternatives: he could stand practically alone as a defender of nationalism while less courageous men rationalized their positions and compromised their convictions or he could seek safety in silence, knowing all the while that if he remained silent he would keep his freedom but lose his self-respect. Once he had publicly committed himself as an unwavering devotee of German nationalism in Prussia, Schleiermacher's fears became a reality, for as a result of his courage to speak out on controversial national issues in opposition to the government his life was covered with a cloud of fear and persecution which lasted for fifteen years.

The first issue in which he became involved was the question of union between the Reformed and Lutheran confessions in Prussia. No other issue could have touched the very roots of his beliefs on nationalism as profoundly as did this protracted controversy, for some of his earliest nationalistic statements had been related to the role of the Church in the state. A brief review of Schleiermacher's ideas on the union of the two church bodies reveals that as early as 1799 he had stated that he rejected "that exclusiveness of the letter which keeps the two chief branches of the Protestant Church apart."[19] He desired to see a union of the Protestant faiths because very early in his contemplations on the relationship between the Church and the state he recognized that there could hardly be any possibility for German unification just on the basis of political agreements. Prussians would first have to settle theological differences which dated back three hundred years to the Reformation before they could reach the place where they would look upon one another as equals. If Prussians could not settle their theological differences within Prussia,

[18] Franz Schnabel, *Deutsche Geschichte im neunzehnten Jahrhundert*, IV, 335.
[19] Schleiermacher, *Sämmtliche Werke, Zur Theologie*, I, 364.

then certainly it would be out of the question to believe that Prussia and other German states would ever be able to agree upon decisive theological differences. In other words, if the Protestants of Prussia could not reach an understanding they could not expect to work out serious differences between the Protestant and Catholic states. Combining the two leading Protestant groups in Prussia would thus constitute a vital part of any scheme to bring about German unification.

Whether he was discussing the settling of questions between Protestants and Catholics or between factions within Protestantism, Schleiermacher steadfastly maintained that the only possible way to achieve a workable union of religious groups in Germany was for the union to arise out of the mutual trust by all concerned.[20] One of the main reasons for Stein's appeal to Schleiermacher during the years of Prussian reform from 1806 until 1808 was that both saw the value of Church union on a freely motivated basis. Being a man of sincere religious convictions Stein was in complete agreement with Friedrich on the point that if attempts were made to stimulate the churches into taking steps leading toward union of the Protestant faiths, the government should be motivated as much by theological considerations as by political necessities. His desire to impart to the churches a strength in unity which they did not possess separately was balanced by a fear of creating a bureaucratic machine in which the churches would become subservient to an all-powerful state. The only item on which the two men disagreed was the method by which the union should be consummated. Schleiermacher wanted to approach the problem of union on a denominational level, whereas Stein felt that it would be more practical to approach the idea of union on the provincial level.[21]

During the whole time that he was following Stein's work so closely Schleiermacher kept uppermost in his mind that only a strong Church could serve the needs of the state. Logically, a Church dominated by the state could be of little value to the state or to its own members. When he agreed to submit a preliminary draft of a constitution for a united German church in 1808 to Stein, this relative freedom of the Church from state control was what he must have proposed. There is no way to tell just what the document contained since Stein evidently destroyed the only copy of the draft when he left office late in 1808.[22]

[20] *Ibid.*

[21] Schnabel, *Deutsche Geschichte*, IV, 321–323.

[22] *Ibid.*, IV, 315; Salo W. Baron, *Modern Nationalism and Religion*, pp. 321–323.

Four years later Schleiermacher submitted to the Prussian government another document entitled "A Project of a New Constitution for the Protestant Church in the Prussian State," which most likely was based on the same material as the 1808 document. In this memorandum he drew the line over which he and the Prussian government would contend for a decade. He readily conceded the point that Church property was derived from the state and was dependent upon the state in a general way. At the same time he vehemently denied that the state held the right to interfere with the internal affairs of the Church. He felt that the state should give the Church so much independence that the Church would appear to be a separate, self-governing body with no connection with the state. He wanted a Church in which the people could express their feelings and emotions as they truly felt them. This was one of the great traditions of Germany. As an integral part of Germany's history, freedom of religious expression would cease to exist under any form of all-powerful state control. One must remember that this was said by Schleiermacher at a time when he was approaching nationalism from a limited and restricted Prussian point of view. Even on that basis he was perfectly consistent as a nationalist in maintaining that the continuity of historical development in Germany depended almost entirely upon the privilege of the average German to express his religious convictions freely.[23] Thus Schleiermacher's support for a union of Prussian Protestant confessions before 1815 was a direct outgrowth of his nationalism. This same nationalism, which had been expanded from a narrow Prussian patriotism to a broad German nationalism, became the basis for his opposition to the Church union after 1815.

On the surface it appeared that the Reformed and Lutheran faiths should have gone together with a minimum amount of difficulty. Both faiths had been able to arrive at a theologically liberal point of view at about the same time. Each confession had only a small fraction which would oppose an act of union. Seemingly the only obstacle in the way of the formation of a single Protestant faith was the working out of an acceptable compromise on the matter of communion—the problem that had held the confessions apart since the days of Luther. Acting under the influence of Altenstein and Hegel, a philosopher who had lately become popular with the King, Friedrich Wilhelm made an appeal to the two confessions in 1817 to celebrate the Jubilee of the Reformation by joining

[23] Arthur Ungern-Sternberg, *Schleiermachers völkische Botschaft. Aus der Zeit der deutschen Erneuerung*, pp. 31–35, 156–157; Baron, *Nationalism and Religion*, p. 138.

in a common confession. The King tried to make it clear that he would not force the two faiths together, while making it equally clear that he considered the union to be an act ordained by God. As far as he was concerned, there were no major obstacles in the way of this proposal.[24]

Schleiermacher's response to the merger proposal by Friedrich Wilhelm was a guarded acceptance. If the King truly intended to combine the two confessions into a single Protestant body without forcing either to accept a doctrine which they did not believe, the first step would be taken in solving some of the basic problems standing in the way of German unification. Here at last was a significant beginning of an effort to make Germany a nation of one nationality and one faith. The only reservation which he had about the merger concerned the course of action the King would take if the two Church bodies were to choose not to unite, for if the King brought force to bear upon the Church bodies he would not only destroy the possibility of the union, but he would also kill any chance for this Church merger to become the basis for general German unification. Feeling that there was too much at stake for Germany's sake for him to oppose the union, Schleiermacher exerted his influence in favor of the merger, an action which was of major significance, for he was president of the Brandenburg Synod of the Reformed Church. The King must have felt a great relief when Schleiermacher led the Synod to approve not only the idea of union, but also the proposed name for the new confession, "Evangelical Protestant Church."[25] On October 31, 1817, Protestant churches all over Prussia exercised the privilege of deciding which of the two practices of communion they would adopt, thus ending a three-hundred-year controversy.

Unfortunately the ease with which the communion question was settled belied the intense struggle which was about to begin over liturgy. As previously noted, Schleiermacher gave his approval to the merger plan because he felt that the interests of German nationalism could better be served by one confessional body in Prussia, but the success of the venture depended entirely upon the freedom given to the Church bodies. Political coercion would destroy whatever value the merger might have for national purposes. Thus, when Altenstein moved to impose a liturgy and a common confessional guide upon the newly created Evangelical Church, Schleiermacher did not hesitate in the least to attack it. He had supported the idea of union in the belief that it would be best for the German nation; he opposed Altenstein's liturgical proposals on the same

[24] Schnabel, *Deutsche Geschichte*, IV, 328.
[25] *Ibid.*, IV, 327–328.

nationalistic basis. In an attempt to make clear his position on liturgies, constitutions, and rituals, he wrote a paper in 1817 in which he expressed some liberal political ideas concerning the implications of the liturgical controversy.[26] He said that a free state ought to have a constitution which reflected the will of the citizens. According to him a monarch had nothing to fear from such an expression of the political feelings of the citizens over whom he ruled, for monarchs ultimately reverted to the will of the governed for their support.

The Berlin theologian further reasoned that the same principle which could be posited for the state could also be applied to Church government. The strength of the liturgy depended upon whether it reflected the theological will of the congregation being governed. By inference he was appealing to the liberal doctrine of democratic elections when he extended the analogy between the Church and the state by saying that the rulers of the Church ought to work for the day when there would be extensive assemblies of elders elected by free community balloting. Going great lengths to show that the clergy were only servants of the Church, he labored to draw a parallel between the Church and the state with an obvious inference: the King was a servant of the people, who could not legitimately impose upon the Prussians what they did not choose to accept. He was issuing a direct challenge to the King and the Chancellor when he maintained that any decision concerning the unification of the Reformed and Lutheran confessions must originate from within the Church circles. In other words, state-imposed decisions were invalid.[27]

These statements by the president of the Brandenburg Synod of the Reformed Church were not the utterances of an aroused clergyman. He was expressing the feelings of a passionate nationalist, who saw the question of liturgy as a superficial aspect of a far deeper conflict. His attack upon the liturgical question was actually a restatement of the right of the people to join with others of their kind in a national state. Whether the question was over liturgy, education, or unification, as long as states like Prussia arbitrarily altered the very basic elements of German culture to suit the temporary needs of the state, a unified German nation would never emerge. Schleiermacher wanted a Church whose life resembled what Humboldt had desired for the development of the culture: a free

[26] Schleiermacher to L. G. Blanc [no place], May 26, 1817, Heinrich Meisner (ed.), *Schleiermacher als Mensch: Sein Werden und Wirken, Familien-und Freundesbriefe*, II, 252.

[27] Schnabel, *Deutsche Geschichte*, IV, 335.

and unlimited evolution along the lines of tradition until all the potentialities of Germany had been fulfilled.[28]

The most distressing fact about the liturgical controversy was that Schleiermacher was one of the few who had the nerve to oppose the government. It seemed that each time he expressed himself with the aim of clarifying his position on any given issue his nationalism caused him to be a nuisance. With each passing day the number of people whom he could call trusted friends grew smaller. He was branded as a liberal, a menace to society, a nonconformist, and a dangerous political agitator.

Undaunted by the personal reverses that he experienced in his battle with the government over liturgy, Schleiermacher was more determined than ever to defend institutions through which nationalism might grow stronger in Prussia. To him the attitude of the Prussian state toward the newly created Evangelical Church was only one aspect of a gigantic, deadly disease which would keep the German body so weak and sickly that no feeling of unity would ever arise. To be sure, Prussia was only one part of Germany but if nationalism could not thrive in the rich cultural environment of that state, what chance was there that less-advanced German states would be able to help unify Germany? The heartbreaking realization for him was that he could not treat the disease but only its symptoms: censorship, forced political thought, and liturgical rigidity.[29]

The difficulties in which he became embroiled with the government were intensified in 1817 and 1818 by events over which he exercised very little control. His problems consisted mostly of word battles with conservatives over issues dating back to the War of Liberation. Considered singly, these "word wars" did not amount to a great deal, but their cumulative effect was disastrous for Schleiermacher when added to the bad publicity which he received over the liturgical controversy.

The most important of these personal controversies concerned a pamphlet written by Professor Schmalz of the University of Berlin, in which Schmalz tried to discredit the Tugenbund. Schmalz denied that there had ever been any extraordinary demonstrations of national spirit by the citizens of Prussia. He lumped all secret organizations and patriotic clubs together as the handiwork of the devil, who worked through perverted minds to achieve his mischief. Schmalz even went so far as to intimate

---

[28] *Ibid.*, IV, 336; Schleiermacher to August Twesten from Berlin, May 11, 1817, Meisner (ed.), *Schleiermacher als Mensch*, II, 249–251.
[29] Schnabel, *Deutsche Geschichte*, IV, 341, 351–352.

that the clamor for a national awakening was really only a disguise for a master plot to overthrow the minor princes of Germany.[30]

Schleiermacher had good reason to look upon Schmalz's attack as a diatribe at himself and others who were trying to keep awake the spirit of nationalism. The presentation to Schmalz of the Order of the Red Eagle, third class, by the Prussian government immediately after he published his pamphlet could hardly be taken by a nationalist like Schleiermacher as a sign of anything besides government approval of what Schmalz had written. Knowing that Schmalz had the support of the King, and also realizing that an attack upon Schmalz would necessarily be looked upon as criticism of the sovereign, Schleiermacher, nevertheless, felt compelled to defend the honor of the men who had risked their lives in the secret societies before the War of Liberation. It was bad enough to see opportunities for free expression of patriotism limited by official disfavor but to remain silent while Schmalz ridiculed and maligned the dead was more than he could do.

Schleiermacher answered Schmalz's recriminations and insults with an open letter entitled "An den Geheimenrath Schmalz," which he made public in 1816.[31] He defended the activities of the secret nationalist societies by attacking Schmalz on three specific points. In the first place, he asserted that the Tugendbund had played a minor part in stirring up a national spirit of patriotism in Prussia. The Tugendbund was a result of Prussian nationalism, not its originator. The patriots who had taken part in the activities of the secret societies in Berlin had been honorable men whose only purpose was to rid Germany of the French invaders and to restore Prussian honor. In the second place, Schleiermacher maintained that the organizations to which he had belonged had been free from the influence of the Freemasons, which was something Schmalz could not say for his own political activities. In the last instance, Schleiermacher stated that the existence of the secret societies had in no way been inimical to the wishes and will of the great mass of the Prussian people.[32]

There can be no doubt that Schleiermacher knew he was wasting his time in even bothering to answer Schmalz's twisted evidence because German intellectuals recognized from the first that Schmalz was advancing groundless charges. Yet, even with the knowledge that he was further identifying himself with the forces on which the reactionaries had vir-

[30] Heinrich Treitschke, *History of Germany in the Nineteenth Century*, II, 365–367.
[31] Schleiermacher, *Sämmtliche Werke, Zur Philosophie*, IX, 645–664.
[32] *Ibid.*, IX, 652–653, 654–659.

tually declared war, Schleiermacher could not sit idly by while the only precious acts of national devotion by the Prussian people were being desecrated by Schmalz. Here again he was placed in a position in which he felt that he had to defend the principles of nationalism as though the nationalists were guilty of some crime. Fortunately for the Berlin theologian and teacher, the King issued an order calling a halt to the controversy over Schmalz and his pamphlet and the whole matter was allowed to die quietly.

The defiant image of Schleiermacher as a militant defender of secret societies was still fresh in the minds of Prussian authorities fourteen months later when the students at the Wartburg Festival burned a copy of Schmalz's work as a patriotic gesture. Here again the weight of circumstances forced the increasingly unpopular Berlin preacher to appear in a bad light. The only time when he had gone on record in favor of anything like the Burschenschaften was when he had sided with Humboldt against Stein to keep the student corporations intact during the reforms of 1808 and 1809. Since the rowdy Burschenschaften had burned some of Schmalz's work, the only conclusion at which one could arrive during the period of reaction was that if Schleiermacher was not a member of some secret student organization, he was at least in complete sympathy with their aims. The irony of it all is that when he was trying to arouse student interest in a patriotic campaign before the War of Liberation he was laughed at by many of the authorities in Berlin. Later, at a time when he had nothing to do with the student gatherings, he was unjustly accused of being part of the illegal student movement.

As could have been expected, Altenstein became so irritated over Schleiermacher's unwillingness to drop the subject of nationalism that he tried to have the King take royal action against the Berlin scholar. In spite of the fact that no substantial charge could be brought against him, only the intervention of Prince Wittgenstein, a Prussian official who had the confidence of Friedrich Wilhelm, saved him from dismissal from the University of Berlin. This brush with Altenstein convinced Schleiermacher of his need to make a clear-cut decision about his devotion to the cause of German nationalism. As he saw it there were only two alternatives between which he could choose. On the one hand, he could rationalize himself into complete silence. He was really accomplishing nothing worth all the trouble he was encountering for the sake of Germany. The German people themselves were not even aware that men like Schleiermacher were championing their cause. The great temptation was to make a public apology for the "mistakes" he had made, retract certain

key statements, and then wait for a climate more favorable for nationalistic agitation. The other alternative was a declaration of his belief in nationalism so clear and precise that the government would either have to
silence him by prosecuting him or accept his views. In doing this he ran
the risk of losing entirely what little influence he had with his Church,
his students at the university, and his close friends, for a man in prison
would be able to do little for the unification of Germany. He finally concluded that if those who believed in the future of Germany did not speak
out, Germany would never exist as a unified nation.[33]

With full knowledge of the repercussions which a vigorous nationalist
"confession of faith" would have, he preached a sermon on October 18,
1818, that was so strongly stated no one could mistake what he was saying. The occasion for the message was the celebration of the victory of
Leipzig, which was a fitting time for making a patriotic defense of nationalism. The sermon was entitled "Rejoicing before God," but was
more of a political speech than a theological discourse. According to him
the main object of the sermon was to free the memory of Leipzig from
the falsehoods which had grown up around it. He felt very strongly that a
great number of the people who were celebrating the famous battle of
the War of Liberation had no right to take any part in the festivities because they had opposed the War. As he stated it, "We know that when
the war was imminent, all those whom we hail as brothers and fellow
countrymen were not of one mind on the great matter."[34] These doubt-
ing and fearful people were certainly different from the true patriots
who had longed for an opportunity to win with the sword what had been
lost by the sword. Forgetting their safety for the sake of the German
people these national fighters learned to live in fear of the unpatriotic
Prussians as much as of the despised French. When the time came for
the campaigns of 1813 to be waged against the enemy, these self-denying
volunteers had almost been forced to proceed against the overt opposition of these fearful and waivering Prussian cowards. When the grand
hour of revolt finally arrived, the same weak individuals who had hindered the work of the nationalists in peacetime had tried to nullify the
sacrifices of the soldiers. Treason was the charge which Schleiermacher
felt obligated to bring against these Prussian weaklings. He insisted that
they should be judged guilty in the sight of man as well as before the
judgment bar of God. To use his words, "But if the events that followed

[33] Schleiermacher to Arndt from Berlin, May 14, 1818, Meisner (ed.), *Schleiermacher als Mensch*, II, 270–272.
[34] Friedrich Schleiermacher, *Selected Sermons of Schleiermacher*, p. 185.

have not changed the opinion of those our brethren, and yet they can take part in the general joy of an anniversary such as this, we must point out to them that theirs is a different joy from the rest, and that it cannot be quite that which the joy before the Lord ought to be."[35]

That some people thought the spirit of nationalism was dead among the masses was well known to him and he denied it in the same lines in which he mentioned it. In answer to such a charge, he asked the question, "Can the rest of us who are met here today thank God for inclining the hearts of men and nations at that time to refuse any longer to bear dishonourable chains, for inspiring them with courage and hope and loving enthusiasm . . . if those sentiments over which we rejoice have no longer the same power in our hearts?"[36] The real victory at Leipzig had been a victory of nationalism over French aggression. If nationalism had subsequently died in the hearts of the men who fought at Leipzig, then it had been a defeat and not a victory.

Schleiermacher could not believe it possible that any man who had known the splendor of patriotism could ever become careless or unconcerned about the future of Germany. If people in Prussia soon forgot the enthusiasm they had known as a nation-in-arms and turned back to the stagnation of pre-Napoleonic times, this was proof that they had only a very superficial notion of what sacrifice really was.

Another group whom he attacked in his sermon were those semipatriotic officials who had served Prussia during the War of Liberation without any real sense of purpose. These halfhearted participants in the conflict were so unstable that they turned upon the government with recriminations every time a lost battle or an unexpected retreat occurred. When there were no disasters over which to worry, these prophets of doom would conjure up some. Schleiermacher expressed the same contempt for these "lukewarm" patriots as Jesus had concerning hesitating Christians. He also assured his congregation that Germany would have been far better off without these superficial patriots who were possessed by "slothfulness and impotence of their own soul, and can neither now nor ever send forth a living shoot of joy."[37] In closing, he turned his attention to the King and his court in the hope that when they decided to punish him for what he had said they at least would have heard the truth concerning the discredited patriotism of Prussia. He said that Prussia had won the war because God had willed that it be so in spite of the numer-

---

[35] *Ibid.*, p. 185.
[36] *Ibid.*, p. 186.
[37] *Ibid.*, p. 189.

ous military blunders made by the allied forces. God had given the people confidence in the ultimate victory of Germany because the national cause for which they had fought was holy and righteous. He very carefully warned the King that this God-given confidence in victory should have been transformed into a willingness to proceed with the natural course of unification.[38]

The pastor of the Trinity Church in Berlin was saying in effect in this sermon that the royal court and most of the men who were in places of authority in 1818 had been guilty of treason because they had not honored the national enthusiasm which God had implanted in the hearts of the people. Knowing that these words would not go unchallenged by the government, he felt compelled to speak out against what he considered to be criminal negligence by his superiors in the Prussian state. He was not sure exactly what action the government would take against him, but he knew that he would not be allowed to say the type of things he had without some type of reprimand. There being no possible room for misinterpretation of what he had charged in his sermon, he could only wait patiently for disciplinary action to begin against him.

If he had preached his sermon against the lack of patriotism in Prussia at any other time besides October, 1818, he might have received the swift and careful attention of the government which he expected. But the weight of circumstances, which so often had seemingly worked against him, now turned events in his favor. The Congress of Aix-la-Chapelle was occupying the attention of the officials of the Prussian government and somehow his latest denunciation went unpunished. Schleiermacher did not know whom to thank for the good luck but he knew it was too good to last.[39] In January, 1819, he wrote to Ernst Moritz Arndt, who was at that time experiencing the first of a long series of difficulties with the Prussian Chancellor. Schleiermacher advised Arndt, who had just married Friedrich's sister, that the life of a nationalist was one of frustration and constant annoyance. If he intended to keep his sanity he needed to shake off his political fears. Rather facetiously he told Arndt that all good things came in groups of three, and that he was still waiting for government action against him to go with his previous troubles.[40]

Throughout the year 1819 Schleiermacher seemed to totter on the

[38] *Ibid.*, pp. 192–193.

[39] Schleiermacher to Arndt from Berlin, December 19, 1818, Meisner (ed.), *Schleiermacher als Mensch*, II, 287–288; Schleiermacher to Gass from Berlin, December 28, 1818, *ibid.*, II, 288–290; Schleiermacher to Brinckmann from Berlin, December 31, 1818, *ibid*, II, 290–291.

[40] Schleiermacher to Arndt from Berlin, January 27, 1819, *ibid.*, II, 291–293.

brink of trouble. The third difficulty which he had told Arndt he needed to complete his set never materialized, although he narrowly missed being dismissed from the University of Berlin over a liturgical dispute involving Altenstein.[41] As the years progressed, and as the Berlin theologian weathered crisis after crisis in the life of the University of Berlin and the Church, he began to tire of his efforts for the sake of what could very well be called a lost cause. The months of anxiety over his career at the University turned into years of uncertainty and it was only in 1824 that he could say with confidence that he no longer feared being dismissed because of his political beliefs.[42] Looking back over the years he had spent not knowing from one day to the next if he would have a position at the Trinity Church or the University, he said that he had done what he had been obligated to do.[43]

During the first few years of the reaction after the Napoleonic wars, Schleiermacher had depended upon the pulpit and the pen in his attempts at spreading the doctrines of German nationalism. Soon he came to see that if he were forced to give up voluntarily his career in either teaching or preaching, he would probably keep his position at the University of Berlin. He arrived at this conviction as he saw the increasing intensity of the reaction in Europe. With each passing day the restrictions upon all normal outlets for political expression grew in direct proportion to the increase of Metternich's influence on German affairs. To the extent that the freedom of expression diminished, so also did the possibility of changing the existing political order fade away. Schleiermacher felt that same sense of desperation which other nationalists experienced as they saw the opportunity for German unity slowly slip from the realm of immediate possibility. The classroom became one of the few arenas for battling the growing lack of concern over nationalistic principles. He determined that he must keep his position at the University at all costs because the hope of future unification of all of Germany lay in the young men who attended his classes. He had to retain his touch with this generation or else surrender in despair in the face of the impossible. So to speak, he saw the lecture as the last hope for the implementation of nationalistic dreams in his time.

[41] Schnabel, *Deutsche Geschichte*, IV, 341.
[42] Schleiermacher to Charlotte von Kathen from Berlin, April 9, 1824, Reimer (ed.), *Aus Schleiermachers Leben*, II, 383–384.
[43] *Ibid.*

During the period of reaction in Germany before 1819 the friction which had steadily increased between Schleiermacher and the Prussian government resulted in nothing more serious for him than a harsh warning by the King. The main reason for the leniency toward him by Friedrich Wilhelm and the government officials in Berlin was evidently the respect which they had for the services he had rendered the Prussian state before the political reaction began. However, the assassination of August Kotzebue by Karl Sand in 1819 and the resulting fear on the part of the Prussian government of a revolutionary outbreak led to a change in the official policy toward any nationalist who insisted upon advocating liberal changes or German unification. Regardless of a man's past performances for the good of Prussia, the King would no longer tolerate nationalist agitation. Also, it should be noted that punishment of political troublemakers was no longer a matter for the King alone. From the time of the assassination of the German writer, Kotzebue, Metternich played a major role in directing Prussia's internal affairs by taking advantage of the excessive fears of the King and his court with regard to liberalism. The near-hysteria in Prussia gave Metternich the opportunity for which he had been seeking: to secure close cooperation from Prussia to prevent the spread of German liberalism and nationalism. By emphasizing the revolutionary character of the Burschenschaften and the obvious unreliability of the university faculties in Germany, the master diplomat of Europe was able to turn the unreasonable fears of the Prussian government into the acts known as the Karlsbad Decrees, passed by the Federal Diet in 1819 and reinforced the next year by the Final Acts.

By the terms of the Decrees the various German governments were required to appoint commissions to supervise classroom instruction in the universities. These commissions could exercise almost unlimited censorship over the lectures as well as over printed matter used in the schools. In addition to the numerous local commissions, a central commission was created in Mainz, its main purpose being to seek out secret societies and to gather evidence which could be used in prosecution of suspected liberals. By censorship, intimidation, and prosecution these commissions virtually controlled the intellectual life of Germany.[1]

Needless to say, with the suppression of liberalism and nationalism in the universities of Prussia following the Karlsbad Decrees, Schleiermacher found that he would not be allowed to make any public defense of nationalism. After the Karlsbad Decrees were proclaimed as the official policy of the government Friedrich knew that he could no longer hope for any type of leniency if he were publicly to renew his fight for a unified Germany. Even if he had wished to continue to preach the values of German unification in defiance of the police, he knew that all the channels of communication which he once had used for nationalistic purposes were so carefully watched and so heavily censored that he could not break the law if he wanted to. The freedom of the pulpit he had once enjoyed as a means of stimulating enlistment in the ranks of the *Landwehr* was gone. Instead, he went into the pulpit of the Trinity Church well aware that his congregation probably held as many government spies as loyal parishioners. The same close official surveillance was duplicated in the classrooms of the University of Berlin, where the Prussian government took even greater pains than in the Trinity Church to see that no inflammatory patriotic doctrines were instilled in the minds of the students. The main difference between the careful scrutiny given him in Church services and the close attention paid by University supervisors to his lectures was that he was actually placed on parole with regard to his lectures.[2] This meant that even the slightest violation of the ban on nationalistic agitation would automatically lead to Schleiermacher's imprisonment, or even worse, to his banishment from Germany.[3]

As a second precaution against the eventuality that he or some other

[1] Alfred Stern, *Geschichte Europas, seit den Verträgen von 1815 bis zum Frankfurter Frieden von 1871*, I, 540–565; Georg G. Gervinus, *Einleitung in die Geschichte des Neunzehnten Jahrhunderts*, I, Part III, 318–518; Georg Kaufmann, *Geschichte Deutschlands im neunzehnten Jahrhundert*, 102–105; Ernest F. Henderson, *A Short History of Germany*, II, 333–338.

[2] Henderson, *Short History of Germany*, II, 334.

[3] Schleiermacher to Arndt from Berlin, July 18, 1823, Georg Reimer (ed.), *Aus Schleiermachers Leben in Briefen*, II, 381–382. See also Friedrich Gentz, "Introduction to the Carlsbad Decrees," in *Europe in the Nineteenth Century: A Documentary Analysis of Change and Conflict*, Eugene N. Anderson, Stanley J. Pincetl, Jr., and Donald J. Zeigler (eds.), I, 74–76.

daring professor might exercise too much liberty with the students, the government banned all liberal or patriotic student organizations. With such a determined effort on the part of the Prussian officials to control the educational processes in the schools, Schleiermacher could hardly have hoped to command a responsive audience even if he had dared to disobey the stern directives of the government concerning the teaching of nationalist ideas.

Because of the presence of spies at his Church services and of commission representatives in the classrooms, he had only three courses of action with regard to his hopes to see Germany unified. First, he could openly defy the government and face certain arrest. Although he had experienced some degree of immunity from 1815 until 1818, he knew that he could no longer expect to remain free if he publicly defied the government. A second possibility was for him to accept the reaction and forget about German unification. The third course of action, which he chose and which he used as his sole means of nationalistic work after 1818, was for him to teach the values of German nationalism to his students but to do it in such a carefully concealed way that the government censors and spies could not possibly take exception to what he said. By transmitting his ideas on nationalism to his students within the context of superficially harmless lectures, he could keep the spark of nationalism alive in the youth of Germany and at the same time avoid the displeasure of the government. The result of this subtle nationalistic indoctrination would be that while no single lecture could be considered seditious the total effect of his series of lectures would be of tremendous value in furthering German patriotism. This indirect method of achieving nationalist goals was a radical departure from the forthright sermons which he had once delivered on the need for loyalty to German traditions, but under the existing circumstances it was all that he could do.

The series of lectures which he used to secretly convey his nationalistic interpretations consisted of a dry, lifeless collection of political discussions which he offered to the students of the University of Berlin under the title "The Doctrine of the State."[4] This title was misleading because he never presented to his classes a complete theory on what constituted a

---

[4] This series of lectures had no consistent organization, nor were the lectures given in any special order. The only extant versions of the lectures were compiled after Schleiermacher's death from the notes of his students and from scraps of notes he left. These lectures were published under the title, *Die Lehre vom Staat*, which constitutes Volume VIII of *Zur Philosophie* of Friedrich Schleiermacher's *Sämmtliche Werke*.

state. He actually discussed a philosophical interpretation of the state as a living organism, which was made up of the total lives, feelings, traditions, and institutions of a nationality within a definite political boundary, which is close to what Boyd Shafer described as the sentiment of nationalism. Shafer, in his book *Nationalism: Myth and Reality,* said that the nationalistic sentiment was an attitude:

... unifying a group of people who have a real or imagined common historical experience and a common aspiration to live together as a separate group in the future. This unifying sentiment expresses itself in loyalty to the nation-state whatever the government, in love of native land however little known, in pride in common culture and economic and social institutions though these may not be understood, in preference for fellow nationals in contrast to disregard for members of other groups, and in zeal not only for group security but for glory and expansion.[5]

All that Schleiermacher did in the way of new interpretation was to apply the nationalistic principles to the state as an organism. This interpretation, which has been called the organic or organismic theory of the state, certainly did not originate with Schleiermacher, having been a fundamental part of the political writings of great thinkers dating back as far as Plato and Aristotle in ancient Greece.[6] Schleiermacher's unique contribution as far as the organic theory of the state was concerned was his application of the theory to nineteenth-century Germany to prove that Germany had progressed through many of the stages necessary to turn a group of people into a nation.[7]

His lectures on "The Doctrine of the State" are therefore most important to the study of his nationalism not only because they represent his final attempt to salvage the ebbing spirit of German patriotism among the youth of Prussia but also because they were his most complete analysis of the part played by social traditions in the creation of a feeling of nationalism. Being the final work of a mature man, these lectures did not contain anything new or revolutionary in Schleiermacher's approach to the problems of nationalism, and, since he had to be cautious with the government censors, they also lacked any radical interpretations. The only significant difference in what he said in "The Doctrine of the State" from what he had mentioned in his earlier sermons and writings was that he had mellowed considerably by the time the lectures were de-

[5] Boyd Shafer, *Nationalism: Myth and Reality,* p. 10.

[6] William Ebenstein, *Great Political Thinkers,* pp. 64–79.

[7] See Francis W. Coker, *The Organismic Theory of the State* and *Recent Political Thought,* pp. 25–27.

livered. Retaining all of the faith he had previously had in the ultimate
victory of German unification, he let his students know very early in his
lectures that a great many things he once had considered imminent in
the growth of a powerful and unified German national would not develop for many years. He refused even to attempt to present a pat solution for the ills which beset Germany because he knew that neither he
nor any other man, for that matter, could project a workable plan around
which a nation could be built. He maintained that regardless of how
perfectly one might devise his political hopes, the plans he drew up for a
perfect state would always be corrupted when men tried to utilize them.
Since even near-perfect ideas would always be corrupted by imperfect
men, the best that any theoretician could hope for under the best of circumstances would be an imperfect master plan for a state.[8]

The keynote to humanity was variation, according to Schleiermacher.
All the efforts at drawing blueprints for states from the time of Plato to
the contemporary efforts of Fichte had been failures because the philosophers usually failed to take into account "the temperaments of individuals who belong to the various acts of the human drama."[9] If no two
men were alike, then how could a philosopher ever hope to make a generalization which would cover the whole realm of mankind? Thus Friedrich excused himself in the lectures from the task of giving to his students
a perfect plan for the creation of a German state. He proposed instead
that his students should consider the state, not as a planned organization,
but as a developing natural product of human intelligence. He assured
them that they really did not need to concern themselves with the problem of the creation of a nation, because whenever any linguistic or cultural group of people came to see that they had a minimum number of
differences and a maximum number of traditional similarities, a nation
would arise of its own force. Neither revolutions, nor party struggles, nor
philosophical speculation could ever be expected to create or duplicate
what only time and tradition could produce.[10] The nation which evolved
as a conscious act of the people would then become a giant organism in
which there would be free-willed participation in the activities of the
state. The total free choices of the whole body of individuals making up
the national state would thus constitute the will of the state.[11]

Schleiermacher's lectures dealt with the nature of the nation and at

[8] Schleiermacher, *Sämmtliche Werke, Zur Philosophie*, VIII, vii-viii, 1.
[9] *Ibid.*, VIII, 1.
[10] *Ibid.*
[11] *Ibid.*, VIII, viii–ix, 80–83.

the same time with the contemporary subject of nationalism by demonstrating that the first moment of consciousness of its own existence by any society is the birth time of a nation. Once a society comes into existence, national development depends solely upon the increase in the degree of consciousness of their own existence by the people of the nation. The more elevated a society's abstract self-consciousness becomes, the higher the governing principles of the nation become.[12] Even though at this point Schleiermacher was dealing specifically with the origins of nations in ancient times, the implications for his own day were unmistakable: Germany would become a nation the day that Germans became conscious of a unifying social heritage. The War of Liberation had not produced a unified German nation because the people of Germany had not at that time attained the national consciousness necessary to form a nation. Furthermore, Schleiermacher maintained that in 1817 the people of Germany had progressed so little politically that instead of looking upon a common government over all the German states as a means of drawing the people of the small states together they thought of the government as "an act of necessary evil, an establishment for security against unrest from without and within, creating and maintaining a lawful condition."[13] By rejecting a fundamental method for gathering all Germans into one body, the Germans had indicated that their political consciousness was shallow and undeveloped. He maintained that the citizen, instead of wanting to be free from the interference of a national German government, should desire a form of government which would be broad enough to cover the "totality of life."[14] The elements of the state which had been deemed necessary by political thinkers before 1817 would automatically be included in this unified result of a national consciousness. Obedience to the law would be a result of the personal consciousness of each citizen that the law is an expression of the people of the nation, thus making the law an extension of each citizen's will. Under this guiding principle obedience to the law would be a natural phenomenon instead of an artificial creation imposed upon an unwilling and frightened population.[15]

He characteristically avoided designating any particular set of customs as "good" or "bad" since each society develops in its own unique way because of its own peculiar degree of consciousness. To call any

[12] *Ibid.*, VIII, ix.
[13] *Ibid.*, VIII, 3.
[14] *Ibid.*, VIII, 7–8, 90.
[15] *Ibid.*, VIII, 92–94.

specific system "bad" would be to negate the principle of the development of national consciousness. What might be good for one nation in one stage of national development could quite possibly be bad for another nation at a different level of progress. The various forms or types of governments—democracy, monarchy, aristocracy—were not to be judged ethically since each results or occurs at certain stages in the growth, development, conquest, or subjugation of all people.[16] According to Schleiermacher, the only valid ethical judgments were those leveled against the society whose national consciousness was reflected in the type of government which that society had chosen. He was re-emphasizing his often-expressed belief that it was a waste of time to try to change the spirit of the German people by altering their form of government. He felt that once the proper growth of national consciousness had been achieved, the changes in government would come about almost automatically. This explains why he had been able to remain loyal to Friedrich Wilhelm of Prussia at the very time when the King seemingly stood in the way of the unification of Germany.

Instead of designating types of government as good or bad, he ranked them according to the degree of national consciousness required by each. Democracy was the lowest form of expression of national consciousness since it was the starting point from which tribes, clans, or small societies began their evolution toward a mature, civilized society. The main weakness of democracy was the danger that people might remain forever on this elementary level without ever developing the comprehension of natural developmental processes of a truly united people.[17]

The next logical step after democracy for a nation was pictured by him as the development of an aristocratic form of government. He was explicit in his contention that this step came only as a result of the progressive development of political consciousness, not because of an expansion of the perimeters of small states for the purpose of physical enlargement. For Schleiermacher national growth was always a matter of vertical growth, never a horizontal.[18] Whether the result of this growth was a small degree of unity within a confederation or a great degree of unity in the framework of a centralized state, higher national consciousness always led to the accumulation of the legislative, judicial, and executive authority in the hands of fewer and fewer people.[19]

[16] *Ibid.*, VIII, xi–xii.
[17] *Ibid.*, VIII, xii.
[18] *Ibid.*, VIII, 14–15.
[19] *Ibid.*, VIII, xii–xiii, 22–26.

The ultimate attainment of any society was the monarchical state ruled over by his version of Plato's philosopher king. For the Berlin lecturer the source of all freedom and justice was to be found in the monarch who had discarded every private interest in order to personify the spirit of all the people over whom he ruled without ever becoming inaccessible to them.[20] Thus democracy was the primitive, aristocracy the intermediate, and monarchy the final state of national development.

The key to understanding Friedrich's arrangements of states in an ascending order from democracy to monarchy was the need which he felt for completeness. He had a compulsion to define the points of origination and termination of every activity undertaken by people. His desire to have a clear understanding of the source of the religious experiences of the Moravian Brethren had been a contributing factor to his disavowal of the Moravian ministry. Later the romanticists drove him to study ancient history and the classics out of a desire to find the sources from which the traditions of his own generation had evolved. The desire to see clearly the beginning and the end of human activity, when applied to the art of governing a nation, was what made him declare that only in a monarchy would there be a clearly defined relationship between the governors and the governed. The delegation of authority under the system of monarchy which had evolved as a factor in national political consciousness moves from the people to the king. At the same time, the execution of laws which express the traditional will of the people is a responsibility entrusted to the king. As far as Schleiermacher was concerned, the highest development of any nation was that level which it would attain when it had a "true" king who expressed in his acts a consciousness that he ruled by the consent of the people.[21]

In the final analysis, the principle which Schleiermacher defended was that unity must prevail in a nation. Whether in the lowest degree, the democratic state, or in the highest degree, the monarchical state, the one thing that all forms of the nation possessed was a unity of the people.[22] Logically, whatever "caused" the unity of the people also "caused" the nation. It also followed logically for Schleiermacher that the only source of true unity was a personal consciousness of nationality by the individual citizen. To prove this point he referred to the system of laws and their enforcement. He suggested that there were only three reasons why people of a nation obey their laws. They may do so out of

[20] *Ibid.*, VIII, xii, 36–37.
[21] *Ibid.*, VIII, xiii, 47–48, 80–82.
[22] *Ibid.*, VIII, 22.

fear that disobedience will bring forth swift and terrible punishment. If fear is the motivation for obedience, then the nation cannot last for any length of time because the same fear which caused the citizen to obey will eventually cause him to change the law by force. A second reason for obedience to the law is the power of tradition. Some people obey the law because they never considered the possibility that any other course of action lay open to them. The third reason for obedience is closely akin to the second, for Schleiermacher believed that people could also obey the law because they loved and respected the legal institutions of their nation. In the last instance the citizen recognizes that the law is an extension of his own feelings. Laws cannot exist unless they are actually the written form of the customs of the people who are to obey the law. As states pass from the level of very limited to very complete political consciousness they have always elevated their customs by placing the sanction of society upon them in the form of a legal code. In deciding to obey the law the citizen utilized two entirely different nationalist characteristics. First, he was acting as a free individual in deciding whether he should obey a law which had evolved from tradition. According to Schleiermacher, no form of law except one based on nationality gave to the citizen this opportunity to decide whether he should obey or disobey a particular law; his decision itself became part of the total will of the people and thus became an integral part of the traditions of the people. In that way every time a man made an ethical decision concerning the law he decided both as an individual and as part of the nation.[23] Schleiermacher used this type of approach to show that since law reflected the customs of a nation, a nation could exist only where the customs were general enough to have the force of law. Nationality, being as it were a combination of factors such as language, customs, religion, and folk tradition, was the only foundation upon which any law could exist.[24]

He made a strong case for his contention that the past pattern of national development indicated that Germany would eventually become a strong, unified nation with a limited constitutional monarchy.[25] As he saw it, no form of government except monarchy could result from the cultural base from which the new German state would have to be produced. However, Friedrich cautioned his students not to be so anxious to see change that they would tend to read into passing events encourag-

[23] *Ibid.*, VIII, 22–23.
[24] *Ibid.*, VIII, 7–9, 20–22.
[25] *Ibid.*, VIII, 26–27.

ing signs that did not even exist. He himself had been guilty of this during the War of Liberation and had learned from the experience that
one should develop a realistic attitude of careful observation of current
events. He specifically pointed out certain developments in Germany
which would serve as indicators that a national consciousness was matur-
ing in Germany.

One of the indicators of such development would be the change of attitude in German people concerning migration. Migration, which in the
past had been an attempt by Germans to better themselves, would become a conscious effort by Germans to better the homeland by extend-
ing its cultural frontiers to other parts of the world. Germany would no
longer export Germans; she would export Germanism.[26]

Another factor reflecting national maturity among Germans would
be their attitude toward the economy of the German states. In the economy of a nationality approaching maturity the aim of monopolies, sub-
sidized businesses, and special-privileged groups would be to work for
the good of the whole nationality instead of for the economic interests
of the limited number of people within the group. The beneficial results
of the business activity of a national economy would always be negated
as long as the basic control of the production and accumulation of profit
resided with a portion of the society which did not possess the characteristics of the nationality. Schleiermacher flatly asserted that any segment
of the economy which did not serve the best interests of everyone comprising the German nationality had no place in the German nation.[27]

Still another development in Germany which would indicate that the
Germans were approaching unification would be the increase in opportunity for advancement in business and government on a basis of ability
and not heredity. He readily admitted that families which possessed
land had a sense of stability, which in turn imparted a degree of stability
to the nation. He was also willing to concede the point that many families in Prussia enjoyed a higher level of life than they could expect if
they had no connection with the land. But he was equally quick in adding
that there were also multitudes of people in Prussia and the rest of Germany who had a definite lack of loyalty to the institutions of their society
because of the absence of the pride of ownership. England had quite
cleverly solved this problem by dividing the legislative functions between
the House of Lords and the House of Commons, enabling the English
people to develop a new tradition of loyalty and family prestige which

26 *Ibid.*, VIII, 97–98.
27 *Ibid.*, VIII, 97–101.

had no relationship to land ownership. The House of Commons became the object of the same kind of pride by the landless that property had been for years for the landed classes. The pride of the people as part owners in the nation through representation in the House of Commons could in Schleiermacher's opinion conceivably be substituted for the pride of immediate ownership of property in Germany, which in turn would open a whole new life of public pride and service for talented but landless German citizens.[28]

Finally, the Berlin professor concluded that Germany would demonstrate her arrival at the doorstep of national unification in the field of commerce when all the states in Germany could settle their tariff problems and create a single German economic unit. He did not have to look very closely into the economic policies of the German states to see the crippling effect those policies had on both the trade between particular states and that between German states and foreign powers. The elimination of the hindering factors which served to prevent the development of a vigorous internal trade would constitute a major step toward unifying all of Germany politically.[29]

In the course of the lectures Schleiermacher made a great many statements that seemed to answer specific questions asked by his students, often making allusion to the fear he had that Germany might try to follow the path taken by revolutionary France. The question which always seemed to haunt him was, "How soon will Germany arrive at the state of national consciousness necessary before a nation can be created from German particularistic states?" The danger was always present that those who were enlightened enough to see the trend in Germany would grow impatient and try to hurry the process of natural development with armed force or social upheaval. To be sure, no man in Germany wanted more ardently to see the birth of a unified Germany than he did. At the same time, no man in Germany was more determined to see the German nation come into existence as a result of the political and cultural consciousness of the German people. The tragedy of the French Revolution was its attempt to move from one type of government to an entirely different kind without waiting for the necessary political consciousness to catch up with the political changes. The same disaster which had fallen upon France would be the lot of Germany if the people tried to unify Germany by force of arms without first achieving political maturity.[30]

[28] *Ibid.*, VIII, 106–110.
[29] *Ibid.*, VIII, 111–112.
[30] *Ibid.*, VIII, 112.

Had he lived to see the explosive period of revolution in 1848 in Germany, he would most likely have told the leaders that the revolution was a mistake.

For those who grew impatient over the slow pace of the spread of nationalism as he himself had during the War of Liberation, the Berlin theologian offered some consolation. The movement from particularism to centralization was already well along the way to completion. If this slowly unfolding tradition of progressive change was to survive, each change in attitude favorable to a centralized Germany "must produce another relationship, under which the public consciousness can no longer remain as it has been."[31] No longer fearing that the German nation would never be born, he was only concerned that it might be brought into existence prematurely. After all, a new German state would have to overcome the opposition of the privileged classes, who would shrink from making a final surrender of their favored positions. The desire of people to retain their particularist loyalties instead of accepting the leadership of a single ruling house would also be a problem. This type of opposition could be overcome only by instilling a devotion to the nation in the youth of Germany. If this was done properly, it would not matter to them who the man was who occupied the nominal position of leadership as king, for he would be only symbolic of the nation.[32]

Schleiermacher's lectures on the "Doctrine of the State" were his last serious effort to keep nationalism alive in Prussia. If one considers the handicaps and limitations under which he lived after 1819, there was really nothing else that Schleiermacher could have done. Keeping in mind that he was a mild-mannered man who did not have a natural tendency to become involved in controversial issues, and remembering that virtually all national agitation ceased in Germany during the reaction, he probably had done as much as any man could have been expected to do for Germany.

Although during the last few years of his life Schleiermacher did not lose his sense of dedication to the cause of nationalism, he noticeably altered his feeling in regard to the need for urgent action to bring about German unification. He came to see that the most significant element in the realization of his national goals was the factor of time—an element over which he had no control. Feeling as he did that he could not speed up the normal processes of development of a national consciousness in Prussia or the rest of Germany, and believing that perhaps gen-

[31] *Ibid.*
[32] *Ibid.*, VIII, 122–125.

erations would pass before the necessary environment arose for the creation of a German nation, he simply withdrew from all controversies concerning nationalism. During the last five years of his life he even expressed a weariness over the whole question of nationalism and the need for defending it.[33]

The irony in his belief that the passing of time would solve Germany's problems was that time also solved many of his own problems. For instance, in January, 1831, he was decorated with the Order of the Red Eagle, third class, in honor of the years of service he had rendered at the University of Berlin—an honor which he immediately interpreted as a sign of the royal favor of which he had so long been deprived.[34] He was literally overjoyed with the prospect of again being an accepted member of the "inner circle" of Prussia after having been ignored for so long by the better people of his country. People who once had been close to him but had been forced to terminate their relationship with him because of the displeasure of the government once more began to drop around to his home.

Of course, a number of things besides the return of government favor were causing Friedrich to forget about the problems of nationalism in the last years of his life. The old physical ailments which had plagued him all of his life returned with more regularity as he grew weaker and weaker physically. Also, as he grew older he had the feeling that he had "done his part" for the cause of German nationalism, and that it was time for someone younger and more agile to carry on the struggle to make Germans see their common heritage. Probably most discouraging of all was the almost complete public apathy toward German unification, which was enough to make even the most ardent nationalist grow tired of trying to do the impossible. Lastly, Friedrich Schleiermacher had come to accept the deterministic point of view that when Germany was ready for a national awakening and a unification effort nothing could prevent it. He did not know when this would be, but he was sure that things would somehow "work out." The result of all these influences was that he finished his life as a nationalist in almost the same manner in which he had begun it: with many ideas and hopes but with no practical plan for his own day and his own generation.

The full effect which the years of fruitless nationalistic effort had upon

[33] Schleiermacher to Charlotte von Kathen from Berlin, December 18, 1827, Reimer (ed.), *Aus Schleiermachers Leben*, II, 434–435.

[34] Schleiermacher to the King of Prussia [no place, no date], *ibid.*, II, 444–445.

the Berlin theologian and teacher could be seen in the complacent manner in which he expressed his ideas on nationalism. Probably the best example of his desire to forget about the entire problem was in a letter which he sent to the editor of *Le Messager des Chambres* in Paris in 1831. This paper had mentioned Schleiermacher's name in a number of articles dealing with contemporary politics in Prussia and had evidently praised him rather highly for his nationalistic efforts. He wrote to the paper in an attempt to correct what he felt was a false image which it had created of him. Since this letter is the last existing document dealing with his relationship to the Prussian state, the King, and the cause of nationalism in general, it is desirable to quote it extensively here. It reads:

Sir, — As it has pleased one of your correspondents in this city to refer to me often, I trust that you will allow me space in your columns for the following answer to what he has said, if for no other reason than for the sake of your German readers.

First, I have to renounce the surname of great, since in Germany we use that name so seldom that it could hardly be applied to a man like myself, except perhaps in trying to ridicule that person, and I do not believe I deserve that.

Second, I am equally far from being "the most outstanding preacher in Germany" as I believe you have stated it, and my sermons cannot possibly be models of eloquence, since I never write them before delivering them. To even attempt to be sublime as a minister would be against my beliefs. . . .

Third, We pray every Sunday that God will grant the king such wisdom as he needs for the fulfillment of the duties which God has delegated to him. But when we do this we are not aware that we express any other "wish of the people" than that it may lead a peaceful life under the rule and leadership of the king, and draw ever closer to the hope of Christian perfection. Such, sir, is the expression of the Protestant Church and I have never diverged from it.

Fourth, It is quite true that I was "forbidden for a time to preach" but it was from my doctor that the order came.

Fifth, I belong to no party of the Left. Your expressions such as right and left, right centre and left centre, are quite foreign to our relations. If your correspondent had been a Prussian, he would not have used terms which do not apply to us. More especially, he would not have spoken of a party of the Left which is secretly intent on revolutionary theories. We have made great progress since the peace of Tilsit, and that without revolution, without chambers, and even without liberty of the press, but the people have always been with the king and the king with the people. Under these circumstances, would not a man be mad to pretend that we could progress more rapidly by means of a revolution?

As for me, I shall always be on the side of the king, and as such will be on the side of the most enlightened men in the nation.[35]

Although he did not deny any of his former beliefs in this letter, Friedrich certainly made it clear to the editor of the French journal that as a Prussian he was loyal to the King and the government which then existed in his country. The fifth section of the letter was in perfect keeping with what he had often said about the need for a slow, developmental process toward national unification, but he seems to have given up all hope of even a near-distant change in the political structure of Germany. On the other hand, to say that he had never expressed any notion in the pulpit except loyalty to the King and his court seemed to be a fabrication. In sermons, both in 1813 and 1818, he had taken some pretty healthy cuts at both the King and the leading members of the government, but this was the very thing that he was trying to forget in 1831. In his zeal to convince the government of his loyalty, or perhaps because of his advanced years, he conveniently remembered events in a slightly different way from which thay had actually occurred.

Probably the saddest commentary on Schleiermacher's career as a nationalist was given by himself in a letter to his wife in September, 1832, only seventeen months before his death. The occasion for the letter was the wave of revolutions which had swept Europe in 1830 and 1831. Expressing deep hurt that the German people would have to go through revolutionary activities before their best interest could be satisfied, he told his wife, "It often makes me sad to think, that after all our bright hopes and good beginnings, I shall, when I depart this life, leave our German world in such a precarious state—for this will most probably be my lot."[36] He knew that he would never live to see the beginning of a new era of cooperation and unity in the Germany he had loved and honored. It is sad to see a man work for a lifetime in pursuit of a goal, and then see that man approach death with the knowledge that all of his work has produced no visible results.

On February 15, 1834, the people of Berlin paid their last respects to the man who had become the symbol of the spirit of national devotion in Germany, in spite of his desires to remain in obscurity. As the coffin bearing Schleiermacher's body was carried through the streets of Berlin

[35] Schleiermacher to the editor of *Le Messager des Chambres*, from Berlin, March 8 [1831], *ibid.*, II, 445–447.
[36] Schleiermacher to Henrietta Schleiermacher from Berlin, September 5, 1832, *ibid.*, II, 469–470.

by twelve University students, a mile-long line of mourners joined over one hundred coaches filled with notables to pay tribute to the dead theologian. The King and the crown prince joined the rest of Prussia in recognizing that Schleiermacher had been one of those people whose life represents the moral and intellectual feelings of the entire nation. By paying him their last respects, the King, the people, the Church, and the country all gave a final recognition to the ideal which had made him what he was.

A close study of Schleiermacher's development as a nationalist brings out several important facts concerning his life and the evolution of a nationalist in general. The first and perhaps most obvious conclusion one must draw is that to be a nationalist a person does not have to see immediate tangible results of his efforts on behalf of his nationality. Since he is working for an ideal which may lie in the distant future the fact that he does not achieve instantaneous success is irrelevant. Scheiermacher was like most other nationalists in that his nationalism, as an emotional approach to German unification, was simply not subject to the same measurements of success as political campaigns or reform efforts. His work for the sake of nationalism continued year after year in the face of strong opposition and without any rewards or visible achievements; yet he steadfastly continued to believe that the goals he sought would be realized ultimately in Germany. All he could bring forth as evidence that he was not wasting his time was that the various German states, because of common customs, habits, and language, belonged together in one country.

In addition to the fact that Schleiermacher had a strong nationalistic faith common to nationalists, one must also note, as a second conclusion, that he had a tendency to interpret nearly everything in the light of his nationalistic convictions. The very fact that a man has chosen to devote all his efforts to bringing about an improvement in the political position of his nationality indicates that nationalism is the single most important factor in his life. Once Schleiermacher decided that German nationalism was the most important and vital cause to which he could devote his efforts, nationalism became an obsession with him. When the nationalist sees one avenue of service closed to him, his determination to improve the position of his nationality causes him to look upon the obstacle in his path as a challenge instead of a defeat. When Schleiermacher was stymied by government censorship in the pulpit and in his lectures he did not give up in hopeless resignation. Instead, he accepted the challenge of government censorship as a mere hazard to be avoided. During his years of efforts to arouse a patriotic awakening first in Prussia and then in all of Germany he tried five entirely different methods of communicating his beliefs to the people. He preached nationalistic sermons; he delivered scholarly lectures; he repeatedly risked his life on dangerous missions which would help free Germany from France; he used his journalistic talents to try to stimulate the national consciousness of the German people, and he even served in the government of Prussia in an attempt to reconstruct the educational system so that nationalism might be advanced. Such resourcefulness in the face of public apathy and official opposition revealed the depth and determination of his devotion to the cause of German nationalism.

A third conclusion one must draw from a study of Schleiermacher's life is that his nationalism was a product of catastrophe and dismay. Each time he gained a little clearer insight into the nature of the problems confronting Germany, he did so because a personal or national crisis forced him to focus his attention on political questions. He moved from cosmopolitanism to individualism, from individualism to Prussian particularism, and from Prussian particularism to German nationalism like a man being driven by an unalterable chain of events, over which he had no control. Realizing little of the joy that should have come to a man who had just made a great discovery, he made the transitions from less to greater national consciousness as though nationalism were a mechanism of escape. This tendency to become more nationalistic under pressure is brought into bold relief by the moderation of Schleiermacher's ardor shortly before his death. As the tension which had developed in Prussia as a result of the reaction lessened, so did his willingness to make nationalism an issue. Though it may not be true in the case of every nationalist, Schleiermacher's life as a nationalist seems to indicate that nationalism thrives best when there is imminent danger or active opposition to the nationality.

The last generalization which ought to be made concerning Schleiermacher's nationalism was that in many ways it was a political ideal sought as a substitute for a solution to his unhappy personal circumstances. In retrospect his whole life was a series of situations in which he was out of place. His early life lacked that warm family affection which seems to constitute a vital part of the life of any normal youth. The modern psychologist might say that Schleiermacher lavished upon his nationality the love and adoration which he would have given his parents and his family under normal circumstances. With his unstable family situation behind him he went to Barby as a youth to study Pietism. Here again he remained on the fringe of the group, never really accepting the Moravian theology of his teachers but never rejecting it either. When he left the Moravian environment to study philosophy he began a fruitless search for a principle around which he could orientate his life. Studying rationalism and Kantian thought proved to be as futile an effort to establish a life philosophy as the study of Pietism had been for Schleiermacher, for he simply was not ready to commit himself to be a disciple of a philosophy which could not meet the basic needs of mankind. As a direct result of his disappointments over the lack of stability which he found in rationalism Schleiermacher formed a friendship with a group of men who seemed for a while to offer to him an understanding of man and man's problems—an understanding for which he had been searching since his childhood. The romanticists excited him, stimulated him, inspired him, but they never captured him, for the differences which separated him from these intellectual companions were too great to be overcome even with the most strenuous efforts. One must remember that his first two great literary achievements, *Speeches on Religion* and *Soliloquies,* were written in an earnest attempt to show the romanticists that he was not so different from them after all.

If he felt out of place among the romanticists, his misery was compounded by his inability to find satisfaction in his various ecclesiastical duties. His views were so liberal that he was never able to realize the personal satisfaction which he knew he should enjoy as a servant of the Church. As a partial solution to this dilemma Schleiermacher sought acceptance by serving his Church in the role of an educator at the University of Halle, only to see even this chance of service denied him when France claimed Halle as a prize of war. During the confusion which followed the war in 1807, he caught a glimpse of the inherent worth of the German traditions as he saw his homeland humiliated by France and Russia. He turned all his efforts to the work of building a resistance movement against the French during their occupation of Prussia, thereby again placing himself among the few instead of the many. When he was finally able to discard Prussian particularism and give his allegiance to German nationalism Prussia was already caught in a reactionary spirit. Once again he was out of step with the majority. This was his fate until his death in 1834. Who can say in the final analysis whether he had too clear an insight into the needs of the age so that he was constantly ahead of those who could see less clearly or whether he was so detached from reality that he demanded that which was always just beyond reach?

Even if Schleiermacher had never lived, it is quite possible that German nationalism would have taken the same strange course through the nineteenth and twentieth centuries. Certainly he was not the father of nationalism in Germany, for many others were calling attention to the patriotic responsibilities of the German people at the same time that Schleiermacher was busily engaged in preaching nationalist sermons at the Trinity Church in Berlin. He did make a clear imprint upon the character of German nationalism, however, by identifying the national awakening in Germany with the spiritual responsibilities of the German people. No other man worked as hard as he did to show that every element of the nation, especially the Church, must be utilized to stimulate the devotion of the citizen for his country. He was likewise one of the first to show that the national character of any group of people was determined by all their customs and that religion was as much a national trait of the German people as their language or their folkways. He did not go as far as the twentieth-century nationalists in making nationalism a substitute for religion, but he must accept part of the responsibility for beginning the trend in that direction by elevating nationalism to a level equal to religion.

In any case, as Friedrich Ernst Daniel Schleiermacher participated in the beginning of perhaps the most powerful movement in Europe in the past two centuries, the greatest impact of his service for Germany was upon his own life. Nationalism gave his life meaning and direction and through his patriotic activities he himself came to know the full measure of the national devotion that a man can have for his homeland, his traditions, and his heritage.

BIBLIOGRAPHY

PRIMARY SOURCES:

Anderson, Eugene Newton, Stanley J. Pincetl, Jr., and Donald J. Zeigler (eds.), *Europe in the Nineteenth Century: A Documentary Analysis of Change and Conflict.* 2 vols. New York: Bobbs-Merrill Co., 1961.

Arndt, Ernst Moritz. *Ernst Moritz Arndts sämmtliche Werke,* edited by Heinrich Meisner. 6 vols. Leipzig: Karl F. Pfar, 1893–1902.

Dilthey, Wilheim. *Wilhelm Diltheys gesammlte Schriften.* 12 vols. Berlin: B. G. Teubner, 1835–1869.

Fichte, Johann Gottlieb. *Fichtes Leben und literarischer Briefwechsel,* edited by Immanuel Herman Fichte. 2 vols. Leipzig: F. A. Brockhaus, 1862.

——. *Johann Gottlieb Fichtes nachgelassene Werke,* edited by Immanuel Herman Fichte. 3 vols. Leipzig: Mayer and Müller, 1845–1846.

Humboldt, William. *The Sphere and Duties of Government,* translated by Joseph Coulthard. London: Chapman, 1854.

Klein, Timotheus (ed.). *Die Befreiung 1813, 1814, 1815. Urkunden Berichte, Briefe; mit geschichtliche Verbindungen.* Munich: W. Langewiesche-Brandt, 1913.

Korner, Joseph (ed.). *Briefe von und an August Wilhelm Schlegel.* 2 vols. Zürich: Amalthea Verlag, 1930.

Meisner, Heinrich (ed.). *Friedrich Schleiermachers Briefwechsel mit seiner Braut.* 2nd ed. Gotha: Perthes, 1920.

——. *Schleiermacher als Mensch: Sein Werden und Wirken, Familien- und Freundesbriefe.* 2 vols. Gotha: Perthes, 1922.

Reimer, Georg (ed.). *Aus Schleiermachers Leben in Briefen.* 4 vols. Berlin: Perthes, 1858–1863.

Schleiermacher, Friedrich Ernst Daniel. *Briefe Schleiermachers,* edited by Herman Mulert. Berlin: Propyläen Verlag, 1923.

——. *The Life of Friedrich Schleiermacher as Unfolded in His Auto-biography and Letters,* translated by Frederica Rowan. 2 vols. London: Smith, Elder and Co., 1860.

——. *Sämmtliche Werke,* edited by Georg Reimer. 31 vols. Berlin: Georg Reimer, 1834–1864.

——. *Selected Sermons of Schleiermacher,* translated by Mary Fredrica Wilson. New York: Funk and Wagnalls, 1890.

————. *Soliloquies,* translated with notes by Horace Leland Friess. Chicago: Open Court Press, 1926.

————. *Werke Schleiermachers,* edited by Herman Mulert. Berlin: Propyläen Verlag, 1924.

SECONDARY SOURCES:

Alexander, Thomas. *The Prussian Elementary School.* New York: Macmillan, 1919.

Anderson, Eugene Newton. *Nationalism and the Cultural Crisis in Prussia, 1806–1815.* New York: Farrar and Rinehart, 1939.

Aris, Reinhold. *A History of Political Thought in Germany from 1789 to 1815.* London: George Allen and Unwin, 1936.

Baron, Salo Wittmayer. *Modern Nationalism and Religion.* New York: Meridian Books, Inc., 1960.

Barth, Karl. *Die protestantische Theologie im 19. Jahrhundert.* Zürich: Evangelischer Verlag, 1852.

Bauer, Johannes. *Schleiermacher als politischer Prediger.* Giessen: Töpelmann Verlag, 1908.

Brandt, Richard. *The Philosophy of Schleiermacher.* New York: Harper, 1941.

Coker, Francis William. *Recent Political Thought.* New York: Appleton-Century Co., 1934.

————. *The Organismic Theory of the State.* New York: Columbia University Press, 1910.

Dilthey, Wilhelm. *Leben Schleiermachers.* Berlin: Georg Reimer, 1870.

————. "Schleiermachers politische Gesinnung und Wirksamkeit," *Prussische Jahrbücher,* X (1862), 234–277.

Ebenstein, William. *Great Political Thinkers.* New York: Rinehart and Co., 1951.

Engelbrecht, Helmuth Carol. *Johann Gottlieb Fichte.* New York: Columbia University Press, 1933.

Ergang, Robert. *Herder and the Foundations of German Nationalism.* New York: Columbia University Press, 1931.

Gervinus, Georg Gottlieb. *Einleitung in die Geschichte des Neunzehnten Jahrhunderts.* 8 vols. Leipzig: W. Engelmann, 1853–1856.

Hayes, Carlton Joseph Huntley. *Essays on Nationalism.* New York: Macmillan Co., 1941.

————. *Nationalism: A Religion.* New York: Macmillan Co., 1960.

————. *The Historical Evolution of Modern Nationalism*. New York: Macmillan, 1931.

————. "Contributions of Herder to the Doctrine of Nationalism," *American Historical Review,* XXXII, No. 4 (July, 1927), 730–731.

Haym, Rudolph. *Die romantische Schule*. Berlin: R. Goertner: 1870.

Henderson, Ernest F. *A Short History of Germany*. 2nd ed. New York: Macmillan Co., 1917.

Holstein, Georg. *Die Staatsphilosophie Schleiermachers*. Bonn: K. Schroeder Verlag, 1922.

Johnson, Robert Clyde. *Authority in Protestant Theology*. Philadelphia: Westminster Press, 1959.

Kaufmann, Georg. *Geschichte Deutschlands im neunzehnten Jahrhundert*. Berlin: Georg Bondi, 1912.

Kedourie, Elie. *Nationalism*. 2nd ed. New York: Praeger, 1961.

Kircher, Erwin, *Philosophie der Romantik*. Jena: Societäts Verlag, 1906.

Kluckhohn, Paul. *Persönlichkeit und Gemeinschaft: Studien zur Staatsauffassung der deutscher Romantik*. Halle: M. Niemeyer, 1925.

Kohn, Hans. *Nationalism: Its Meaning and History*. New York: Van Nostrand, 1955.

————. "Arndt and the Character of German Nationalism," *American Historical Review,* LIV (July, 1949), 789.

Krieger, Leonard. *The German Idea of Freedom*. Boston: Beacon Press, 1957.

Mackintosh, Hugh Ross. *Types of Modern Theology*. London: Nisbet and Co., 1954.

Mann, Golo. *Secretary of Europe: The Life of Friedrich Gentz, Enemy of Napoleon,* translated by William H. Woglom. New Haven: Yale University Press, 1946.

Meinecke, Friedrich. *Weltbürgertum und Nationalstaat: Studien zur Genesis des deutschen Nationalstaates*. Munich: R. Oldenbourg, 1907.

Müsebeck, Ernst. *Ernst Moritz Arndt: Ein Lebensbild*. 2 vols. Gotha: Perthes, 1914.

————. *Schleiermacher in der Geschichte der Staatsidee und des Nationalbewusstseins*. Berlin: Perthes, 1927.

Peake, Samuel. "History of Theology," in *Germany in the Nineteenth Century*. 3 vols. New York: Longmans, Green and Co., 1915.

Pinson, Koppel. *Pietism as a Factor in the Rise of German Nationalism*. New York: P. S. King and Son, 1934.

————. *Modern Germany: Its History and Civilization.* New York: Macmillan Co., 1954.

Pundt, Alfred George. *Arndt and the National Awakening in Germany.* New York: Columbia University Press, 1935.

Reinhard, Joseph. "Friedrich Schleiermacher als deutscher Patriot," *Neue Jahrbücher für Pädagogik*, IV (1899), 345–360.

Schnabel, Franz. *Deutsche Geschichte im neunzehnten Jahrhundert.* 4th ed. 4 vols. Freiburg: Herder Verlag, 1949–1954.

Seeley, John Robert. *The Life and Times of Stein.* 3 vols. Cambridge: Cambridge University Press, 1878.

Shafer, Boyd. *Nationalism: Myths and Reality.* New York: Harcourt, Brace, and Co., 1955.

Snyder, Louis Leo. *The Meaning of Nationalism.* New Brunswick, N. J.: Rutgers University Press, 1954.

Stern, Alfred. *Geschichte Europas seit den Verträgen von 1815 bis zum Frankfurter Frieden von 1871.* 10 vols. Stuttgart: Hertz, 1913–1928.

Trietschke, Heinrich. *History of Germany in the Nineteenth Century,* translated by Eden and Cedar Paul. 6 vols. New York: McBride, Nast and Co., 1919.

Ungern-Sternberg, Arthur. *Schleiermachers völkische Botschaft. Aus der Zeit der deutschen Erneuerung.* Gotha: Leopold Klotz, 1933.

Valentin, Veit. *The German People,* translated by Olga Marx, edited by Dorothy Teall. New York: Alfred A. Knopf, 1952.

Volpers, Richard. *Friedrich Schlegel als politischer Denker und deutscher Patriot.* Berlin: B. Behrs Verlag, 1917.

Wittram, Richard. *Das Nationale als europäisches Problem.* Göttingen: Vandenhoeck und Ruprecht, 1954.

Zeigler, Theobald. *Die geistigen und sozialen Strömungen des neunzehnten Jahrhunderts.* Berlin: Bondi, 1911.

INDEX

Aix-la-Chapelle, Congress of: 142
Alexander I, Czar of Russia: negotiations of, with Friedrich Wilhelm III, 71, 72; and Napoleon, 73
Allied Powers: 116, 124
Altenstein, Baron Karl von: relationship of, with Schleiermacher, 80, 132, 139, 143; on common confession, 134, 135; mentioned, 131
Amiens, Treaty of: 56
anti-Semitism: of Schleiermacher, 114–115
Arndt, Ernst Moritz: relationship of, with Schleiermacher, 115, 142; exile of, 116, 129; on death of Scharnhorst, 119
Arndt and the National Awakening in Germany (Pundt): 5
Athenaeum: 10, 26, 27
Auerstädt: battle at, 57, 60
Auf Scharnhorsts Tod (Arndt): 119
Augereau, Marshal: 62
Austerlitz: battle at, 56, 57
Austria: and German nationalism, 113, 116–117, 123

Barby, Prussia: Schleiermacher's education at, 14–15, 17, 46, 90, 162.
Bartholdi, ———: and *Landsturm*, 104
Barth, Karl: on Schleiermacher, 6
Basel, Treaty of: Schleiermacher on, 57–58; mentioned, 56
Bauer, Johannes: on Schleiermacher, 7–8
Bautzen, Prussia: 112
Bearsch (Prussian patriotic editor): 69
Berlin, Prussia: Schleiermacher in, 23, 66, 75, 99; secret-society work in, 69–70; defense of, 106, 111, 112, 113; Arndt in, 115; mentioned, 45, 52. SEE ALSO Trinity Church of Berlin
Berlin, University of: creation of, 84, 86–88; Prussian patriotism of, 92–93, 137–138, 145, 146–155 *passim*; Schleiermacher at, 96, 121, 129, 143, 146, 156; mentioned, 8

Bernadotte, Marshal Charles: 62
Beyme, Karl von: 54
Bonaparte, Napoleon. SEE Napoleon Bonaparte, 115
Brandenburger Synod: 135, 136
Breslau, Prussia: 13, 110
Breslau, Treaty of: 98–99
Buber, Martin: 114
Burschenschaften: 139, 144

Catholicism: revival of, 27; Protestantism and, 85, 132–133; mentioned, 65
Charity Hospital of Berlin: 23
Charlottenburger Bund: 115
Charlottenburger Verein: 69, 70
Confederation of the Rhine: 57
Congress of Aix-la-Chapelle: 142
Congress of Vienna: 129
Convention of Tauroggen: 96
Correspondent: 118, 119
Cuxhaven, Prussia: 56

Davout, Marshal Louis-Nicolas: 57, 74
democracy: as form of government, 151
Die Staatsphilosophie Schleiermachers (Holstein): 8
Dilthey, Wilhelm: on Schleiermacher, 7
"Doctrine of the State, The" (Schleiermacher): 146, 147
Dreifaltigkeitskirche: 75
Dresden, Prussia: 116

Eberhard (citizen of Halle): 62
education: Church-state relationship in, 36, 76–77, 87; reform of, 75–78, 80–81, 84–88, 92; Zöllner on, 77–78; Stein on, 78, 81, 82; Humboldt on, 78–82, 86–87
Eichhorn, Johann: 116
Elbe River: 56, 57
Enlightenment, the: 41
Erfurt; Convention of: 71, 72
Evangelical Hospital of Berlin: 6

Evangelical Protestant Church: 135, 137
Eylau: battle at, 57

Federal Diet: 144
Fichte, Johann Gottlieb: relationship of, with Schleiermacher, 39, 48; and Prussian educational reforms, 78, 86; mentioned, 9, 10, 148
Final Acts: 144
France: relationship of, with Germany, 88, 91, 96, 97, 101, 105, 106, 118, 131; relationship of, with Russia, 96, 97, 118; and Allied Powers, 116, 124
Friedland: battle at, 57
Friedrich Wilhelm III: role of, in nationalism, 37–38, 100, 103, 107–108, 112, 136, 141–142, 144; and Rumbold kidnapping, 56; against Napoleon, 57, 71, 96; opinion on, of Schleiermacher, 63, 124, 129, 131, 132, 150, 158; and Russian alliance, 71–73, 96, 99–100; and Stein, 75, 82, 83; on education, 87; and *Landwehr*, 104, 105, 111, 119; on Schleiermacher, 120, 121, 139, 144, 159; on confessional union, 134–135, 136; on Schmalz, 138, 139
Froriep (citizen of Halle): 62

Gass, Joachim: 61, 63
Gentz, Friedrich von: 123
German People, The (Valentin): 67
Gneisenau, Marshal Augustus Neidhardt: activities of, in patriotic societies, 69, 115; and *Landwehr,* 104
Goethe, Wolfgang: influence of, 15, 79
Grolmann, Karl W. von: 69
Grossgörschen: battle at, 111
Gruner, Justus: 115
Grünow, Eleanor: Schleiermacher's relationship with, 47, 62–63
gymnasien: 87

Halle, Prussia: 60, 84
Halle, University of: influence of, on Schleiermacher, 15, 17–18; appointment of Schleiermacher to, 52, 54, 55, 162; French occupation and, 61–62, 63, 66; Schleiermacher's sermons at, 63–65
Hardenburg, Friedrich von. SEE Novalis

Hardenburg, Karl August von: 78, 131
Hayes, Carlton J. H.: on nationalism, 3–4, 76, 109
Haym, Rudolph: 7
Hegel, Georg: philosophy of, 10, 134
Herder, Johann Gottlieb: nationalism of, 50, 76, 92
Herder and the Foundations of German Nationalism (Ergang): 5
Herz, Henrietta: 23, 50
Historical Evolution of Modern Nationalism, The (Hayes): 4, 9
Hohenzollern family: 108
Holstein, Georg: 8
House of Commons: 153, 154
House of Lords: 153
Humboldt, Wilhelm von: educational reforms of, 78–82, 86–87; relationship of, with Schleiermacher, 79–82; 86–87; on culture and history, 136–137; student organizations and, 139

Ideas on National Education (Zöllner): 77
individualism: in Kantian philosophy, 18; in Spinoza's philosophy, 19; in *Soliloquies,* 39–41; nature of, 45, 64; in Fichte's philosophy, 48–49

Jacobi, Friedrich Heinrich: 19, 125
Jacobins: 10, 59, 69
Jahn, Friedrich Ludwig: 129
Jena: battle at, 57, 60
Jubilee of the Reformation: 134
jurisprudence: interpretations of, 91

Kant, Immanuel: rationalism of, 17–18, 19, 90; individualism of, 18, 48; Schleiermacher on, 39; mentioned, 9, 10, 59, 162
Karlsbad Decrees: provisions of, 144–145
Kathen, Charlotte von: 124
Kedourie, Elie: 4
Kluckhohn, Paul: 8
Knapp (citizen of Halle): 62
Kohn, Hans: 4
Königsberg: Kant at, 18; Tugendbund at, 69; Schleiermacher's mission to, 71–74; mentioned, 116
Kotzebue, August: 144
Krug, Johann: 69